CHILDREN OF CALAMITY

By *John C. Caldwell*

CHILDREN OF CALAMITY

COMMUNISM IN OUR WORLD

LET'S VISIT FORMOSA

John C. Caldwell

CHILDREN
OF CALAMITY

Illustrated

THE JOHN DAY COMPANY
NEW YORK

Second Impression

© 1957 by John C. Caldwell

Library of Congress Catalog Card Number: 57-5979

MANUFACTURED IN THE UNITED STATES OF AMERICA

Foreword

THIS is a book about children. In every country, among all peoples, children are the greatest national treasure, longed for and cherished by their families and communities. The instinct is sound, for children are the hope for human survival. When the natural environment of family and society is destroyed by war and catastrophe, and above all by war, the children are the ones who suffer most. Then the treasure is wasted and the loss to mankind is severe.

This book, then, is about the world's wasted treasure, the lost and unwanted children, the lonely, the desperate children. They roam the streets of cities. They hide in the ruins of bombed buildings, they maraud the countryside, they live a life of innocent crime. Most of them are orphaned by war, many are fathered by soldiers who desert them or do not even know of their existence, some are the somber fruit of indigenous or accidental poverty.

Whatever the reason for their being, these children exist. They are in our world without their own wish or will, they struggle for life upon our globe. John C. Caldwell has undertaken to find them for us. He has made a journey to discover them and he presents them in their heartbreaking innocence and need. Because they are children he presents them with hope. A few people, he tells us, are doing a great deal to save the lost children. We are inspired by these few, and we are made ashamed because they are so few. Where are all the other good people? Why are we not all helping the children?

There is only one answer possible to the question which will inevitably be asked by everyone who reads this book. We who are many must join the few. The children must be saved. They must be found, they must be taken from their abodes of misery, from the homelessness of the streets. They must be sheltered and fed and healed and taught and above all loved, and so brought back again into the human family.

Yes, John C. Caldwell has lit a lantern and carried it around the world. Its light falls upon the gaunt unsmiling faces of millions of bewildered children, who live in darkness. Tragedy indeed, but not without remedy! These are still children. They can be saved if we who read, we the many, join the brave few who are their saviors and so increase their strength.

PEARL S. BUCK

Contents

Sixteen pages of pictures will be found following page 96

CHILDREN OF CALAMITY

1

The Tunnel of Tragedy

FOR thirty minutes after leaving Tokyo's Central Station the train runs through the vast sprawling city and on into the indistinguishable mass of ugly housing that is Yokohama. Then suddenly the big cities are left behind, the railway abruptly entering the lovely countryside south of Tokyo Bay. On a clear day Fujiyama is visible for miles; here and there the traveler catches glimpses of the sea and lovely beaches.

An hour and a half south of Tokyo by express is the little town of Oiso. Sandwiched between the ocean and the mountains that rise to Fuji's snow-covered peak, Oiso is one of the loveliest spots in Japan. There are numerous summer homes along the bay, and nearby hot springs make of Oiso a year-round resort.

A wooded ridge lies between the railroad and the sea. And through the ridge there is a tunnel, used during the war as an air-raid shelter. The tunnel leads to the summer estate of the wealthy Sawada family and it is locally known as the Tunnel of Tragedy. For in this spot where a rich Japanese family once lived is located the Elizabeth Saunders Home for mixed-blood children. Through the tunnel have walked hundreds of Japanese girls, abandoned by their

American lovers, faced with the problem of raising or disposing of the children left behind.

The Elizabeth Saunders Home is not the only home for mixed-blood children in Japan. There are two other similar homes; there are children of American fathers mixed among the orphans of Japanese parentage in eight other orphanages. But Elizabeth Saunders is perhaps the best. It is supervised by Madame Miki Sawada, who has spent nearly a decade working with what she calls "the innocent victims of war, the abandoned children of mixed American and Japanese parentage." The home is located on the estate where Miki Sawada spent many happy days of her youth. Madame Sawada's husband is a prominent Japanese diplomat. She is a Christian, educated in England. And she probably knows more about the problem of mixed-blood children than any other person in Japan.

The Elizabeth Saunders Home is the best orphanage of its type in Japan. It is the recipient of Sawada family money. Miki Sawada travels constantly, to America and to Great Britain, speaking and appealing for help. The Home also receives help from the Japanese Government and from the Episcopal Church. And 105 Americans are currently sponsoring children at Elizabeth Saunders through the Christian Children's Fund, to the amount of more than $500 each month.

But the problem of mixed-blood children extends far beyond Oiso and Japan. In Korea also there are "innocent victims of mixed American and Japanese parentage." Farther south in Asia there are thousands of mixed-blood children. For colonialism and war have one by-product in common. Both have produced unwanted accidental children. They are found by the thousands in Indo-China, in Southeast Asia, in India.

No one can know accurately how many children have been fathered by combat and occupation troops since 1939. It is estimated that there are a total of 400,000 illegitimate children left in the world as a result of war and occupation. Not all are the responsibility of American soldiers. German soldiers left 8,000 children in Norway and more than 5,000 in Denmark. Other thousands of German-fathered children were left in Holland and Belgium. In Asia, the soldiers of Japan did their share, leaving behind an estimated 75,000 babies in Southeast Asia and the islands of the Pacific.

Eurasians, these children in the Far East have been called in the past. Now frequently the term Amerasians is used. But whatever the name, the children face tremendous problems.

As I stood talking to Madame Sawada outside the home a plain Japanese country girl emerged from the Tunnel of Tragedy. On her back, in the custom of old Japan, was a child. I could not understand the conversation that took place, paid little attention until I saw the woman was crying. And then Miki Sawada did a strange thing. She went to the child, still strapped on its mother's back, and, wetting her finger, rubbed the child's coal-black hair. Immediately the blackness disappeared, in its place a patch of shining blond hair.

Thus, in the midst of Oiso's beauty I came face to face with one of the great human tragedies of post-war Japan. Like many other Japanese mothers, the woman had kept her child's parentage secret by rubbing charcoal dust into its hair. But now the child was thirteen months old, subterfuge would soon be impossible. The mother had come to a difficult decision. The child must be given up.

But even in such circumstances there is love, there is heartbreak, there are tears. For me it was a shocking experience. But for Miki Sawada the drama had been played scores of times. During the past six years while she has cared for more than five hundred mixed-blood children, she has been forced to turn away other hundreds.

"Like so many, she does not even know who the father is," Miki Sawada told me as the Japanese woman walked back alone through the Tunnel of Tragedy. "Sometimes they only know that it was 'Jim from Chicago,' or 'Tom from Korea,' or 'a sailor with a tattoo.' "

There are beautiful children at Oiso, children of Japanese-white and Japanese-Negro blood. There are talented children and idiots. A small trickle move out, adopted by Americans. But a life in America will be impossible for most of the mixed-bloods. Too few Americans are interested, perhaps because the whole problem has been hushed up by American and Japanese authorities. It is interesting to note that among the several nations responsible for mixed-blood children in Asia, only the French in Indo-China show a sense of responsibility. Hundreds of French-Vietnamese children are being shipped to France each month, traveling as French citizens on French passports. The United States Government has even refused to cooperate with the Christian Children's Fund in a project to resettle Japanese mixed-bloods in Hawaii.

How many children have been left behind in Asia by American soldiers? A few years ago an American magazine stated there were 110,000, a figure which Japanese communists eagerly seized upon.

The Japanese Government gives a far lower figure. In 1952 the Japanese Welfare Ministry circularized 5,443 Japanese obstetricians and 38,872 midwives, asking them to give particulars of all children of mixed parentage whom they recalled delivering since 1945. Seventy-seven per cent of the questionnaires sent out were completed, listing a total of 5,013 *remembered* mixed-blood deliveries.

In addition 11,000 U.S. servicemen registered their marriages to Japanese women between 1947 and 1952. Many of these marriages took place after children had been born. In many cases the marriages were conducted according to native Japanese rites and the children thereafter abandoned. Numerous other illegitimate children have, of course, been produced since 1952, when the Japanese Government made its survey.

Miki Sawada estimates that one out of two of the Japanese mothers does not know the identity of her child's father. Twenty per cent of the children are the result of one chance encounter. The child of the mother I watched walk back through the Tunnel of Tragedy was one of these. During the Korean War five hundred American soldiers arrived in Tokyo each day on "R. & R." (rest-and-relaxation leave). Another two hundred arrived each day in Kobe and Kokura. The number is much smaller now, but R. & R. goes on. It is Madame Sawada's opinion that fifty per cent of the mixed-bloods are R. & R. children.

The story of R. & R. is told in an official report by an American army chaplain. The typical soldier on leave arrives at Tachikawa Air Force Base near Tokyo. From the air base the soldiers are taken into Tokyo by bus. Upon arrival each is issued a clean dress uniform, his military currency is exchanged for Japanese yen, he receives PX cards, and is free. Each soldier reaches the street with an average of two hundred dollars in his pockets.

And in the street there is a waiting horde of taxi drivers. The soldier has already been softened up by a sales talk by the bus driver on the way into the city. The taxi driver, who is usually an agent, has little trouble in talking the soldier into a visit to a pre-arranged hotel, and he receives a cut of 10,000 yen for each customer delivered. In many cases the Japanese agents take short cuts. The buses from Tachikawa frequently discharge men at the hotels even before they have been processed. The driver, employed by the U.S. Army, receives 100,000 yen ($275) if he manages to deliver a busload.

The price of a week's lodging in the typical sex hotel is $105. The hotel supplies a Japanese girl for each man for the week for 12,600 yen, or $35. Drinks and tips take the rest of the soldier's money.

For the soldier who does not fall victim to the bus driver or the taxi agents, there is still the hazard of hundreds of pimps and streetwalkers who roam the Ginza and the PX and Tokyo Central Station areas. An American army chaplain estimates that at the height of the Korean War and for many months after Panmunjom the take of the sex hotels in Tokyo amounted to $36,000,000 annually. Now, of course, it is much less.

It is from these contacts that 50 per cent of America's unwanted children in Japan result. The babies still come, will continue to come, mothered by ignorant country girls like the one I saw at Oiso. Many of the girls are sold into prostitution by their own families, the price being as low as $75 in 1956. Japanese procurers roam the countryside working economically depressed areas with especial care. Or they wait at the railroad stations in the big cities, offering a glittering life to the girls who come to the cities for work.

What of the other 50 per cent? These children and their stories are more tragic because there was love, affection, sometimes a long relationship between father and mother.

These are the children of American men and their Japanese "onlys."

James Michener wrote of the love of American men for their "onlys" in his novel *Sayonara*. He visited Oiso in his search for background material. Perhaps he read, as I did, the remarkable documents in Miki Sawada's possession. When children are given up, the mother frequently gives Madame Sawada a packet of letters with such a request as this: "Please show these to my little boy when he is old enough to understand. Then he will know that his father loved me."

In Madame Sawada's living room at Oiso I read the letters of many American fathers. There are letters filled with love, letters of hope and promise, others clearly written to deceive. How much of them most of the Japanese mothers understood is questionable. For around their plight has developed a translation racket. Japanese schoolboys, their own English not too good, translate the letters, charging $1.20 per page. Many of the letters show the marks of honest translators—Japanese ideographs under certain words, other words underlined, or with question marks. But Miki Sawada has seen many translations in which no effort is made to bring out the promise or the hope. And perhaps it is just as well, for the letters inevitably become less frequent, as in the case of J, father of three boys in the Elizabeth Saunders Home.

J was among the first Americans to land in Japan—the oldest boy is nine years old. (American troops landed in September, 1945, and the first mixed-blood child was born in May, 1946. A Japanese radio announced the event and the man who made the announcement was promptly ordered dismissed by American military authorities.)

In all the letters J writes of his "only" as "Mom" and he signs most of his letters "Papa." He might well have been the "Mom's" father, for she was only sixteen when they met. And as is so frequently the case, he was already married to an American girl.

J wrote first from San Francisco, explaining that he could not, after all, get out of the Army.

> I know, my darling, how this letter is going to hurt you, but please dear, don't worry. I am coming back, for as you know I love you and the children more than life itself. Six months seem a long time, but remember, my dear, we have so much to live for. It means, darling, that you must cut down on your living expenses, get rid of the old maid —that will save you 5,000 yen. . . . Give my love to George, Jimmy and David, and to you, my darling, everything that I have in life is yours. You have been the finest mother and the most loyal wife that any man could wish for. . . .

In December, 1951, J wrote expansively of his plans to return.

> I should be on my way back sometime in April. . . . I am sorry, my dear, that I cannot be with you and the children for Xmas, but I will make up for it, upon my arrival. . . . I am enclosing a money order for $30, which, dear, is not much of an Xmas present, but until I hear from my people on the east coast, or until I receive full pay, I cannot send money. However, as soon as possible I will send you plenty, so my darling stop your worrying. We are going to be so happy *when I return*. If you don't hear from me before Xmas, on Xmas night at 12:00 midnight stop and think of me for a few minutes for I'll be thinking of you at the same time. . . . I can still see you

as I left you, that Monday morning at Kamakura. I could not turn back. I wanted to but something told me if I did that you and I both would have broken down. I remember when I kissed you good-bye your lips were cold. . . .

But J's promises to send money regularly did not materialize. And he began to lay the groundwork for desertion. Or perhaps it was military red tape that became ensnarled in honest dreams. For a few weeks later he wrote:

I cannot get out of the army before my time is up, *or for 21 months.* I don't know where in hell the Far East Command got the information that men could be released to retirement before their time was up because it is not true. . . . I know this news is as great a shock to you in as much as you are alone with the three children but, my dear, you must make out some way. I'll send you as much money as I can, which as you must understand is not much. I must continue paying that $147.50 to my ex-wife until her interlocutory decree becomes final, which isn't until next April. . . . I telegraphed my brother but have had no answer. . . . Please don't worry yourself too much. You can sell anything in the house that you choose to if you think it is necessary. Love to you and the children always, my darling.

And J added a little P.S. to this letter:

There is nothing here in America, my darling, except high prices, and very cold-blooded American people to deal with. I have seen no women that can compare to my Japanese wife. I would give, my darling, five years of my life, to be back right now with you and the children. As soon as I hear from you I will send some money.

But evidently J's blood was also getting a bit cool.

Shortly thereafter he wrote his Japanese "wife," urging that she sell all the furniture in order to obtain money. Explaining why he could not help, J wrote:

I have written my brothers several letters, to please pay what is owed me for many years. The answer I got was that they did not owe me one cent. Now, my darling, I'll tell you what I have done, I have written the Adjutant General, and requested that I be reassigned to Japan. I have told him that, if this is granted, I will extend my active military service for one year. I must get back to Japan, to you and the babies. I know how you have been suffering, but my darling, please believe me, I am doing everything possible. . . . As you remember, my divorce becomes final in April, so if I can come back to Japan, we can be married anytime after April 30th. . . . Now, darling, where did you leave George, Jimmy and the baby? . . . My dear, I'll try and explain everything when I see you. I know that you have lost face, but darling, I'll pay every penny we owe, so keep an account of what is borrowed. Are you working? If so, where? Who are you living with and do I know them? What are the rooms costing you? How are you living? Did you owe either of the maids when they left? Honey, please let C write your next letter to me, he can explain in English, so much better than an interpreter. Don't feel bad about selling the furniture, we can get all new furniture when we start housekeeping again.

My dear, when you answer this please tell C everything you have to say, so he can explain to me in the letter he will write for you. . . . Mom, for the love we both have, please wait and keep going. I'll come back, my darling, to you and the children, perhaps sooner than we both expect. All my love, Your husband always.

This was the longest and among the last of the letters J

wrote to Kamakura. Shortly thereafter the curtain suddenly rang down. Three small boys, now aged nine, six and going-on-five, walked through the Tunnel of Tragedy soon after the letters stopped coming. And their mother, still only twenty-five years old, probably did as many of the mothers do—joined the throng of streetwalkers who appear about the Imperial and Nikkatsu Hotels in Tokyo in an endless vigil that begins at dusk and often does not end until dawn.

There are many other letters in Miki Sawada's collection. There are letters from "Somewhere in Korea," from military bases, country towns and large cities all over the United States. There is a letter from a "mother-in-law" in Kansas to Tomie in Tokyo:

> Now, Tomie, please answer these questions in your next letter. Where do you work? What do you do? How much do you make? How many hours a week do you work? Who takes care of the boys while you are away? How much do you pay for taking care of them while you work?
>
> I suppose you think that it is none of my business but darling I need to know these things to be able to help you and I am doing everything possible to help. Jimmy came over the other night and I had a good long talk with him and I laid your condition down to him and as he is young and didn't realize what it means to raise a family alone I got him to promise to send some money each month to be used on the boys. . . . We do not see too much of Jimmy as he is working long hours trying to earn a little money to get the boys over here which is going to be a long-drawn-out affair because of so much Govt. red tape. Did you ever talk to the American Red Cross about getting them in? Tell them that their father and grandparents are willing and anxious to receive them. . . . Now, Tomie, I hope that you can understand this letter. I love you, dear brave

little girl. Love to all three of you from your mother in the U.S.A.

It is doubtful if dear, brave little Tomie understood about government red tape. Perhaps there were the best of intentions on the part of a Kansas couple. Perhaps J too had good intentions, and gave up because he became snarled in difficulties. But Tomie soon had to give up the struggle and her two boys walked through the Tunnel of Tragedy.

There are other letters from mothers and sisters in America, indicating that a surprising number of mixed-blood fathers told their families about the children left behind. There is a series of letters from a graduate of an Ivy League university and there are letters from uneducated colored boys who themselves need interpreters.

There are cold and harsh letters, like one from a boy in Alabama who ends his relationship by writing, "Be letting me know how the boy is doing. Sure would like to see you both. Maybe some time we can meet again. Bye, Bill."

And there are also letters from a few men truly suffering from remorse. A series of letters from a man in New England, covering a period of over two years, ends on this note:

My dearest Mitsuko, I haven't heard from you since the spring of last year. How is little Sylvia, I do hope that she is well and it seems to me as though you would have dropped me a line as to how she is getting along. . . . I have regretted the things I didn't do when I had a chance a thousand times over. Mitsuko, I've made a terrible mistake. . . . Oh, my darling, is it too late? Are these words falling on deaf ears? Oh, Mitsuko, how I have wronged you and my heart as well. It is written that a man should follow his mind and his heart. Darling, not only have I wronged you and Sylvia, I have wronged that which a man's life must be ruled by—his heart . . . If there was only someone I could open my heart to, but darling there is no one. Oh, Mitsuko please, I beg you try and find it in your heart to forgive me. I know that it is much too late. I remember you wrote once that man's life is transitory, how right you are. But, darling, the Lord will make a way for you and Sylvia. I am more than likely out of His favor. But darling, I hope to regain it.

Perhaps young E in New England was right. The Lord did guide Mitsuko to Madame Sawada. But it is doubtful that E regained any lost favor. For his remorse was forgotten. The stream of little checks he had sent soon ceased.

But E was not unusual. Only one father has ever continued to send money after his child or children entered Elizabeth Saunders. The one exception is a Negro soldier, serving a life term for murder. He has not forgotten.

One American soldier wrote Madame Sawada from Korea asking for help.

Dear Mrs. Miki Sawada:

With a happy heart and great pleasure I write this letter. I don't know exactly how to start what I want to say. I was stationed in Japan for two years. I had a friend which we had contacts for about a year or so. In 1949 a baby was birthed by this friend. Which month I can't remember. I had only seen the baby a few times. He was so little then and now I couldn't recognize him. He had the name "Little Lucky" then. Now, I don't know. Getting to the point, I would like to have him if he is not wanted. I am not married but I have two parents. We have had several talks together. In fact they want him more than I. I can assure you, he will have a nice home and someone to love him and not mistreat him. I hope you will contact me if you have any news of his whereabouts. I would like to take him back to America with me when I leave Korea.

Unfortunately there were five thousand-odd children and "Little Lucky" could not be found. The problem was complicated by the fact that the corporal from Korea had forgotten his "friend's" name.

It is such stories that have made Miki Sawada a little bitter. Certainly the official attitude of the United States, in contrast to that of the French Government, has not been helpful. Red tape has probably kept a number of children from a decent life. Three hundred-odd children have been adopted and are now living in America. But for most this is impossible. In a little booklet she has prepared to help raise funds, Miki Sawada writes:

> By the time the girl found herself pregnant her *hero* disappeared and her old feudalistic parents cast her out as a dishonored daughter . . . homeless and jobless she wandered about. Some like her managed an abortion but those who could not afford it decided, after the birth of the fatherless child, to leave the innocent that some merciful hands might pick it up. . . . We earnestly hope that you of their fathers' country will help these children. Let us share our responsibilities together. We grownups started the war. Let us not make these innocent children suffer any more.

Certainly we can agree with Madame Sawada that the children are innocent victims of a war and occupation they had no part in creating. And it is not possible to condone the actions of an American father who leaves three children in Japan. But the blame cannot be placed on the shoulders of Americans alone.

The same feudalistic parents who cast their daughters out when they become pregnant by an American sometimes sell their daughters into the very life which eventually produces the unwanted children. The whole attitude of post-war Japan on the matter of sex is involved. Tokyo is to my knowledge the only city in the world where streetwalkers enter the best hotels, linger about the lobbies, and openly go to guests' rooms. The only regulation: they must either be out by eleven or spend the whole night.

Tokyo, with its myriad streetwalkers, pimps, private sex shows, strip teases, and pornographic studios, openly exploits sex. Four blocks from the venerable and still swank Imperial Hotel there is a section reserved for deaf-mute prostitutes who specialize in perversions. It is a loathsome experience to walk along the street at night, for the pedestrian receives no protection from the several Japanese policemen who stroll about.

Putting it bluntly, Japan is utilizing its women to bring in foreign exchange. The mixed-blood children are the victims of the Japanese way of life as well as of American promiscuity. But whatever the blame may be, it should be possible to help the relatively few children who have become the victims.

The problem is first to see that several thousand children of American fathers receive decent care, good food, proper medical attention in qualified homes like Elizabeth Saunders. This can be achieved if one hundred times the number of Americans who now sponsor mixed-blood children through the Christian Children's Fund or other organizations will carry the small load of $10 a month per child.

Only six hundred children are in institutions where they belong. The rest are being cared for by their mothers and under increasingly difficult and even hostile conditions. Hundreds of children are living with relatives, their presence considered a disgrace.

But there will remain bigger problems. The Japanese are antagonistic toward the children; most of them will have little chance for happiness in their own country. A few years from now, when hundreds of the mixed-bloods will be completing high school, there will be the problem of making a living. If these children, most of them attractive and mentally alert, cannot go to Hawaii, they must be sent to some part of the world where there is a need for new blood, where discrimination because of race and color is not a problem.

Madame Sawada thinks she has found that place. Last year she went to Brazil, found the authorities interested, and took an option on fifty acres of land. She is bringing a young Brazilian couple to Japan, to work in Elizabeth Saunders and become acquainted with the children and their problems. Eventually Miki Sawada hopes to send her graduates to Brazil where their talents are needed, where they will have a chance for a wholesome life.

But a much larger program than anything Madame Sawada can handle will be needed to meet the problems of the years ahead in Japan. It is probable that other Latin American nations would be interested. It is possible that all of the mixed-blood children could be settled in the Americas. But if this is to happen, money and leadership are needed. Miki Sawada cannot do the job by herself.

Seiji Giga, Executive Director of the Christian Children's Fund in Japan, lists a number of additional problems that must be met if the plight of Japan's unwanted children is to be improved.

He believes the first problem is to help children still living with their mothers or other relatives. Many of these should be in institutions. In other cases the greatest good can be accomplished by rehabilitating the mothers, giving them vocational training so that they will be able to earn a respectable living and can gain some sense of security.

As to the children in institutions, Mr. Giga believes the greatest help would be to find sponsors who would be willing to see them through college. Many of the children, born early in the occupation, are already past the age when adoptive parents can be found. For these children there must be either an education abroad, or jobs abroad.

Seiji Giga lists as a third major problem the future of the children of Negro fathers. "It is my own opinion," says Giga, "but I feel these children are going to have an especially hard time in Japan from now on."

And finally there is the problem of the mentally retarded or physically handicapped children. In one orphanage in Japan I saw one of these unfortunate children, of Japanese-Negro blood, chained to his bed like an animal.

"One solution to this problem," says Giga, "is to gather together all these abnormal or subnormal children in one place and look after them, but here again many problems will arise."

The greatest of these problems is money—and interest— on the part of Americans. The Sawadas and the Gigas need help. The American Joint Committee for Assisting Japanese-American Orphans has helped in finding foster parents who will legally adopt these children. But the Refugee Relief Act which provides that four thousand war orphans from all parts of the world may be brought to America for adoption was to expire in December, 1956. Henceforth, unless the law should be extended, each adoption will require a separate act of Congress.

The future of from five to six thousand mixed-blood children can be made secure, but only if there is far more imaginative and aggressive planning than has been the case in the past. The Japanese Government is spending over

$100,000 annually on the children. The American Government is spending nothing.

Seiji Giga is not as bitter as Miki Sawada about America's lack of interest. He says simply, "Now that the problem is seen to be much smaller in magnitude than was originally thought, perhaps the generosity of people in the United States and of the servicemen in Japan can be augmented to form a fair share of the cost of providing for these fatherless children."

The Christian Children's Fund of Richmond, Virginia, the organization whose activities Seiji Giga directs in Japan, is doing more for the mixed-blood children than any other American organization. But support of more than one hundred children in Miki Sawada's home and others in eight general orphanages in Japan is but a small part of what CCF is doing all over the world, wherever fatherless and needy children are found.

During 1955 and 1956 I visited orphans and orphanages supported by CCF in fifteen nations on three continents. I traveled by jeep over the rugged roads of Korea, by car into the Indo-Tibetan border regions, by Dyak longboat down the muddy rivers of Borneo, by reindeer sled across the frozen lakes of Lapland. I saw children orphaned by communist aggression, unwanted children of mixed parentage in half a dozen lands, children who had been sold into slavery, children abandoned on the streets.

This book is the story of children I have seen, talked to, played with. And it is the story of a remarkable organization, staffed by remarkable men and women, which with the help of thousands of Americans each giving $10 monthly to support a child overseas, is creating a future for children who otherwise would face a life of beggary or humiliation.

2

"Rush Five Hundred Orphans"

SEVERAL times a year a strange cable message flashes from Richmond, Virginia, across the Pacific to Hong Kong. "Rush me 500 orphans," it may read, or "Need 200 Korean, 10 Japanese mixed-blood, 50 Chinese, 10 Arabs." The cable sets into motion a flurry of activity on the sixth floor of an office building on Hong Kong's Nathan Road, the Christian Children's Fund's overseas headquarters. If the order for orphans is not too large, it is filled from the bulging files there. If sufficient applications and case histories are not readily available, other cables go from Hong Kong to Seoul, Korea, to Japan, to Singapore, Jerusalem, Naples, or Calcutta.

On one memorable occasion the cable from Richmond ordered the staggering total of 2,400 Korean orphans.

Thus in a typical week, five-year-old Keiko, mixed-blood child of Japan; five-year-old An Hua-sil of Korea; eleven-year-old Wang Yu-ching of Quemoy Island, and seven-year-old Talaa, an Arab boy, joined the enormous family of the Christian Children's Fund. Each child suddenly had a home, and an American foster parent paying $10 monthly for support, writing letters, sending gifts.

Little Keiko and her mother walked through the Tunnel of Tragedy at Oiso. An Hua-sil, abandoned in a Korean railroad station, weighing just twenty-four pounds, entered the Christian Children's Home at Anyang, Korea, where 205 orphaned children live in Asia's first cottage-plan home.

Two thousand miles to the south, Wang Yu-ching was found by an American army chaplain in a Quemoy village smashed by communist artillery. Yu-ching had already experienced her share of bitterness, having been sold as a slave. And the communist shell which crashed into her Quemoy home crippled her for life. Wang Yu-ching, minus one leg, found her way to the Wego Home in the lovely hot springs town of Peito, Formosa.

Talaa, the Arab boy, was picked up starved and wandering, on the slopes of Lebanon's Mount Herman. Brought to the one hundred-year-old Schneller Orphanage at Khirbet Kanafar in Lebanon, Talaa began a new and exciting life. For he had never been inside a house, had never slept in a bed, had never seen a stairway, had never worn shoes.

During the past decade an average of two homeless children have joined the CCF family each day, acquiring an American foster parent, a home, a guarantee of care and education. That guarantee extends to the time when the child has completed school, been trained for a job, or is married.

The Christian Children's Fund operates in thirty-one countries, its homes stretching from far below the equator in South America to two hundred miles inside the Arctic Circle in Finnish Lapland. Twenty-seven model orphanages have actually been built by CCF. And where other organizations are in the field, but need assistance, CCF moves in to help. CCF-sponsored children live in 179 orphanages operated by such diverse religious groups as the Russian Orthodox Church, the Church of England, the Mennonites, and the Methodists. Thus by mid-1956 CCF was operating or helping to operate a total of 206 orphanages. CCF is an interdenominational missionary organization, caring for children regardless of race or creed. It is the largest Protestant child welfare organization in the world.

CCF operates agricultural experimental farms, runs trade schools, gives courses in welfare to social workers, publishes three welfare magazines in Korean, Chinese, and Japanese, produces food for its children and frequently enough additional to sell, manufactures textiles, furniture, shoes, toys, produces oil of citronella, makes uniforms for soldiers and fine embroideries for sale on the market.

April, 1956, was a typical month for CCF. During that month the Bott Memorial Home in Tokyo, a model cottage-plan orphanage and child welfare center, was completed. Ten thousand miles away in Jamaica, CCF took on the support of a home for the untainted children of lepers, and a home for blind children, both to be operated by the Salvation Army. In Belgium it completed an agreement with the Mennonite Church to assist in the management of a new home. In Puerto Rico plans were completed for a forty-five-acre farm and model home. Twelve thousand miles across the South Pacific in the jungles of North Borneo CCF took on the sponsorship of all eligible children in a struggling orphanage operated by the Methodist Church.

And April was not a month of unusual activity, either for CCF or for Calvitt and Helen Clarke, who founded the organization in 1937 and have guided it throughout its nineteen years of existence. As is so often the case in an outstanding philanthropic work, CCF is the lengthened shadow of one man, a monument to his vision, a fulfillment of his dreams. Or in the case of CCF it would be more accurate to state that the monument must be to the man and his wife. For the Clarkes have worked as a team in building CCF into a world-wide Boys'—and Girls'—Town.

J. Calvitt Clarke is an ordained Presbyterian minister, a graduate of Western Theological Seminary in Pittsburgh. During World War I he went overseas to do work in Russia but ended up working with Russians in France. When he returned to the United States he began to look for a pastorate. And while looking, he took a temporary position with the Near East Relief Foundation.

Nearly forty years have passed and "Champ" Clarke has still not found a church. The temporary Near East Relief job lasted a decade. Then Clarke became one of the three founders of the Save the Children Federation, this work to be followed by a stint helping Helen Keller, raising money for work in the southern mountains of America, and another money-raising job for relief activities in Puerto Rico.

It was outside a barber shop in Chambersburg, Pennsylvania, in 1937 that Calvitt Clarke had the vision that has been transformed into the Christian Children's Fund. Clarke, the Presbyterian minister without a church, met a Methodist missionary just returned from China. The Methodist told of problems in China, of Japanese aggression and brutality, of thousands of children left homeless in the wake of armies, after air raids, artillery bombardments.

"Things must be very bad—especially for children," said the Presbyterian.

The Methodist replied, "Well, you have had a lot of experience in helping people overseas. Why don't you do something about it?"

The Presbyterian looked through the window of the clean barber shop, down the pleasant streets of prosperous Chambersburg, and thought how different must be the wretched poverty of war-stricken China. And he answered,

"I will." A month later the first remittance was cabled to China.

Calvitt Clarke had returned to his home in Richmond, talked to Helen about China. Together they prepared a little circular, went to a printer, and guaranteed to pay for the printing. They advanced money for the first mailing of a thousand copies. And then, because the Clarkes realize the necessity of control and organization, they went to friends and neighbors, asking them to serve on an executive committee. It is typical of the manner in which Calvitt Clarke operates that he took these steps *before* he had collected a dollar. For his motto has always been, "Stick out your neck and trust the Lord."

The first mailing produced a remarkable $700—enough to pay the printer and the postage with enough left over to cable a very sizable remittance to a bombed-out orphanage in Kukong, a refugee center in South China's Kwangtung province. In the nineteen years that have passed since Calvitt Clarke first stuck his neck out, he has collected the staggering total of $30,000,000 for the world's unwanted, starving, and lonely children.

CCF, its first work limited to China, was incorporated as China's Children's Fund. T. Nelson Parker, Richmond attorney and later mayor of the city, became the chairman of the executive committee. Mr. Parker is still chairman of today's greatly expanded CCF.

Soon there was enough money to restore the badly damaged Kukong Orphanage, to take in five hundred children. Then the American Embassy and a group of missionaries in Peking asked Dr. Clarke for help. CCF began to help five homes in that ancient city. At the end of the war, CCF was operating all through China and shortly thereafter moved into Burma and the Philippines.

When the Communists took over China, CCF was operating forty-five orphanages with physical property worth over one million dollars.

But even with China gone, the needs of children all over Asia were staggering. Dr. Clarke explains his philosophy in these words: "We are like a doctor, who even in the middle of the night will get up and attend to a patient, feeling that this is his job."

And there are millions of patients who need the kind of doctoring CCF is giving children, scattered almost from the North to the South Pole. Soon after the fall of China, cries for help came from Japan, Korea, India, the Middle East, Europe, South America. As the responsibilities of CCF increased, it became necessary to set up an overseas headquarters. Hong Kong was selected because thousands of Chinese refugee orphans are there and a large proportion of CCF orphans and its activities are in Asia.

But unlike many other relief organizations, CCF has no other branch offices. It must, of course, maintain headquarters in countries where it supervises many homes. But administratively CCF is operated from Richmond and Hong Kong. There are no offices elsewhere in the United States or Canada, no expensive professional fund-raisers, no drives for money.

The continued growth of the Christian Children's Fund is due to several factors. The Clarkes believe that the tremendous problems of children throughout the world preclude any narrow, denominational approach. CCF will give help to a home operated by any missionary organization, provided it can be assured that the children grow up in a Christian atmosphere, with proper food, medical attention, and schooling.

Originally viewed with suspicion by many denominations, CCF now has scores of missionary-financed homes on its waiting list, asking for help. In addition to monthly subsidies for the children, CCF will build new facilities, provide needed equipment—everything from toys to refrigerators.

Thus in the Philippines, CCF built "Children's Gardens," a model cottage-plan home operated by the Methodist Church and caring for one hundred children. In Lebanon, CCF built one of the finest schools in the country, as an adjunct to an orphanage operated by the Swiss Reformed Church.

In 1956 CCF was co-operating with twenty-nine different religious groups. The demand for further assistance can be indicated by the fact that in Korea alone, 140 orphanages have asked to be taken under the Clarkes' wing. Where the need is great, Calvitt Clarke has helped non-Christian groups. In Korea he stuck his neck out very far, taking on the responsibility of helping an orphanage supervised by a devout and practicing Buddhist. It is not to the credit of Christian people that this action caused considerable criticism.

Another factor in the success of the organization is that it has maintained a remarkably low overhead. During 1956 approximately twelve per cent of funds received went into administration. The orphans got the rest. This figure is remarkable inasmuch as it includes the cost of world-wide supervision which in 1956 included two round-the-world trips, two separate trips to Europe and two supervisory trips to Central America and the Caribbean area. And finally it also includes the cost of appeal advertising, the method by which CCF finds the Americans willing to pledge $10 each month to sponsor a child overseas.

But the greatest factor in the success of the Christian

Children's Fund is the manner in which both Calvitt and Helen Clarke have developed the sponsor–child relationship. I have not been able to ascertain who first used this "foster parent" plan. Calvitt Clarke disclaims any credit for the idea. It is used now by a half dozen organizations. But none have used it in the same personalized manner developed by the Clarkes.

Each month advertisements appear in leading magazines describing the plight of a specific child, asking for Americans who will sponsor that child, or other equally needy children. Sometimes an advertisement brings in poor returns. In other cases the picture of the child, with Calvitt Clarke's simple story, touches off a tremendous response. One advertisement showing a starved Korean child, belly bloated, arms and legs like match sticks, brought in nearly $500,000.

When an American family, or individual, or Sunday School, or club answers an advertisement, agreeing to sponsor a child, the Clarkes go into action. The overseas office in Hong Kong supplies a picture, complete biographical data if available. The new sponsor gets a long, personal letter from Dr. Clarke. Soon he begins to get letters from the child, badly written, or often poorly translated. The letters keep coming, and soon a flow of correspondence is established between an American in Iowa or South Carolina and a child in Korea, Hong Kong, or Bethlehem.

Helen Clarke is in charge of adoptions and largely responsible for the relationships that have developed between sponsor and child. Calvitt Clarke gives simple testimony to Helen's effective work, saying, "We have had almost a miraculous growth. A great deal of credit, at least fifty per cent, belongs to Mrs. Clarke, who has peculiar and unusual talents in composing letters, in keeping in touch with

the people who hold adoptions. Right now she works until two or three o'clock some mornings."

But the most effective testimony is that in 1956, among
more than 18,000 adoptions, there were only 600 drop-outs.
No one is obligated to continue sponsorship. The payments
can stop after the first $10. But most sponsors carry
on year after year, learning to love their overseas child,
hanging its picture on the wall, sending birthday gifts and
Christmas packages.

As more and more Americans travel, especially to Asia,
sponsors drop in to visit their children. This year a hundred-odd Americans will visit their "adopted" children in
Hong Kong. Some sponsors show remarkable initiative in
getting to off-the-beaten-track places. In October, 1955,
a little Anglo-Indian mixed-blood girl was made happy
when her sponsor from Florida dropped in unexpectedly
at the Graham Homes in Kalimpong on the Tibetan border. Even a seasoned traveler has some difficulty in getting
to Kalimpong. But Mrs. Christine Beakes of Maideria,
Florida, found her way to the Graham Homes and thereby
gave a lonely little girl a thrill she is still talking about.

Helen Clarke's biggest job is preparing the "Christmas
material." Each Christmas every sponsor receives a long
personal letter from the Clarkes; a letter from the child,
in original language and an English translation; a printed
Christmas card; another card drawn, or painted, or
scrawled, by the child. The work of preparing the Christmas material must begin months in advance. Thousands of
individual letters must be written and from overseas come
18,000 more letters, written in fourteen different languages.

It is little wonder that both Calvitt and Helen Clarke
must work seven days a week and sometimes sixteen hours
a day. It has been necessary for them to give up their

lovely farm in the Virginia countryside, to spend most of their time in CCF headquarters on Richmond's once swank Second Street. Now the fine old homes have largely become business offices or boarding houses. In two connecting structures, appropriately named the "China Building," Calvitt and Helen Clarke work and live for their orphans.

But the eighteen years of work have had wonderful rewards. "Champ" Clarke will probably never get his church now, but he has thousands of youngsters all over the world. Hundreds of sponsors have come to know him personally, as a friend and counselor. He gets appeals for advice, on marriage, divorce, business affairs. A constant stream of letters pours into the China Building from every state in the union. Sponsors call from far-off cities, asking if it is too late for a Christmas package, or why little Kim in Korea hasn't written, or what is the best way to get to the Casa Materna in Naples or the Fanling Babies' Home in Hong Kong.

But perhaps the greatest thrill and reward come when the Clarkes visit CCF homes abroad. In 1955 they had planned a trip, but Helen fell and broke her hip. As soon as she was allowed out of the hospital and could hobble about on crutches, she insisted that the trip be made. The Clarkes went around the world, to be greeted by thousands of children, many of them awed at seeing the Clarkes in person. They received gifts, saw skits and plays, heard specially prepared songs, watched athletic contests. And everywhere they went, Helen Clarke hobbled in and out of every dormitory, every kitchen, every cottage, asking questions, taking notes, planning how CCF could enlarge its service.

I do not know how many buildings are named after the Clarkes. In Anyang, Korea, there are a "Helen Clarke

Cottage" and a "Calvitt Clarke Cottage." In Tokyo's new Bott Memorial Home there is a Clarke Hall. On the shores of the Malabar Coast of India there is a Clarke High School. And plying the waters of Hong Kong bay there is a motorboat, CCF's *The Lady Clarke.*

Who are the sponsors, who by their gifts of money, letters, and love, make children happy? An adult Sunday school class in Nashville, Tennessee, sponsors four children in Borneo. A farm couple near Council Bluffs, Iowa, have adopted a Korean child. A family at West Newton, Massachusetts, have taken on four victims of communist aggression in a Hong Kong home. A lonely government gal, living in a Washington hotel, has three children in the CCF-affiliated Casa Materna in Naples. The inmates of an institution for the criminally insane in Wisconsin, the staff of a religious magazine in Illinois have adoptions.

There are, of course, many people who cannot afford to invest $10 a month in a needy child. But more and more people of limited means are sharing in an adoption. Last year seven girls—Beatrice Ingliss, Linda Companion, Marion Gast, June LaMotte, Aline Turnage, Betty Christman and Hazel Bishop—all workers in Plant One of the Whirlpool Corporation in St. Joseph, Michigan, adopted Pai Nam Soo, a two-year-old Korean girl.

What happens to the $10 monthly given by the sponsor? A small proportion, averaging 12 per cent, provides for CCF administration which includes two supervisory personnel in the Hong Kong overseas office; an American in charge of the huge Korean operation; a Japanese welfare worker in Japan; a Finnish schoolteacher in Lapland; an Englishwoman in London; and a young American couple in India.

The rest of the sponsors' money goes to the children.

But each child does not necessarily receive the full amount. In some countries CCF is forced to spend several times $10 a month to care for each child. In Lebanon it has spent in building a needed school the equivalent to all the money that will be received from the 126 sponsors of children in the home for the next fifteen years.

In other countries it is not necessary to spend as much per child. Each year CCF makes a cost-of-living survey of each country. It considers the financial situation of the missionary organization with which it is co-operating, the amount the organization lacks to give the children what the Clarkes consider to be minimum care. So in some places as little as $2 a month is spent on each child, in others $50 a month.

And always Calvitt Clarke is willing to take on new burdens, even before the sponsors have been found. He says, "Fifty per cent of the children of the world are undernourished, some of them plain hungry, and in places like India some of them are actually starving. There is no limit to the work Christian Children's Fund can do."

Only a few statistics show the need that still exists in every part of the world. In the Middle East there are 908,000 Arab refugees. Hong Kong, with a normal population of 400,000, is swollen with 2,000,000 refugees. There are 640,000 refugees from Communist Vietnam living in South Vietnam. There are an increasing number of Chinese children, like Wang Yu-ching, orphaned and hurt in the twilight war along the China Coast. There are perhaps 600,000 mixed-blood children resulting from war, occupation and colonialism.

Wherever there has been war there are orphans or other children in need. Wherever there are vast refugee populations there are children needing help. There are large populations of second- and third-generation refugees, victims of wars and persecution which only the older among us can even remember. And even on our own doorstep, in the United States, in Latin America, there are depressed areas, places where children are simply abandoned on the streets.

Any of these children, black, white, yellow or brown, is eligible for adoption, provided the child is under fourteen years of age and is an orphan, or has only a mother who is unable to provide adequate support.

There is no better place to begin the story of today's lonely and unwanted children than in Hong Kong, overseas headquarters of the Christian Children's Fund, a city filled to overflowing with refugees and wandering children, each with a different story of tragedy and heartbreak.

3

China's Children

GO INTO a laundry or restaurant in New York's China-town, ask the Chinese where he comes from, and eight times out of ten the answer will be Toishan. In San Francisco and Los Angeles the story will be the same. Nearly a century ago the people of Toishan, a district of South China's Kwangtung Province, began to come to America, to work on the railways, to go into business, and to become first-class American citizens.

Toishan is famous not only as the ancestral home of most Chinese-Americans. It is an area frequently hard hit by devastating famine. And for some Chinese, Toishan will be remembered for another reason.

During one of its worst famines, and in the midst of war, a twenty-nine-year-old missionary, Verent J. R. Mills, began at Toishan an 800-mile trip that ranks with the 3,000-mile Long March of the Chinese Communists as an epic of human endurance. Verent Mills made his long march, not with hardened and disciplined soldiers, but with an army of children. One hundred and forty-two children began the seven-week journey, 142 finished it. In a master-piece of understatement, Verent Mills says, "By the end of the journey we were covered with lice and not too clean as we had not had the pleasure of a bath in seven weeks, but we were happy to be at our journey's end because it was just about the end of me."

Well it might have been the end of Verent Mills. It began because Toishan was in the path of an invading Japanese army. For two weeks, after leaving the flat paddy lands, Mills' small army climbed through the rugged mountains west and north of Toishan. For six days during this period, Mills carried four children balanced in baskets at the ends of a Chinese carrying pole. The mountains safely crossed, Mills and the children bedded down in the village of Shiuhing, hoping to have a quiet and restful night. At 2:00 A.M. Japanese artillery began to crash into Shiuhing. Unwittingly Verent Mills had blundered into the path of another Japanese advance. One hundred and forty-two sleepy and in some cases sick children were awakened, had to hike more miles through darkness, over another mountain pass, until they reached a river up which they could travel to the safety of Free China.

Verent Mills' long march took place in May and June of 1942, and his story is part of the story of China's children, of the plight that has faced them for a half century. Since my own birth in China at the time of the Revolution in 1913, China has had little peace. After the revolution that deposed the Manchus came years of struggle between opposing war lords. Just when peace seemed possible in the thirties the armies of Imperial Japan struck. And after eight years of war with Japan and while the rest of the world celebrated the peace that seemed to have come, the Chinese faced another five years of internal warfare.

During all these years China's children have suffered, have been a part of huge refugee movements, have been orphaned by the thousand. No one can accurately estimate the number of Chinese children orphaned by war. But Verent Mills, now overseas director of the Christian Children's Fund, can estimate the suffering. Since the sultry day in May, 1942, when he and his children began their long march, the crying of frightened children, the battle to save the ill, the fight to provide homes for the homeless, have been his life.

The tragedy of China's children still goes on, both inside China and off the China Coast. It is a tragedy that can in a measure be understood in Hong Kong, a city of 2,000,000 refugees where the Christian Children's Fund alone supports 2,300 children in ten huge orphanages. And it is a tragedy that can be better understood by going back to Toishan in the years 1942 and 1943 when Verent Mills began his work with Chinese orphans, a work that now extends to the orphans of the world.

Verent Mills was already a veteran missionary in 1942. Born in England and transplanted to Canada at an early age, Mills was supposed to follow in the footsteps of his engineer father. But when he was nineteen years old he heard a missionary speak about China. Fascinated by the story of China's needs, he went back again and again to hear the missionary's story. And finally he walked forward to pledge his own life to missionary service.

Verent Mills' parents refused to take him seriously. They would not sign his passport application. But the pastor of the church Mills attended in Winnipeg signed the application and in 1932, soon after his nineteenth birthday, Verent Mills was in Kwangtung Province, South China. For several years he lived as a Chinese and dressed in Chinese clothing, and he became remarkably proficient in the difficult nine-tone Cantonese dialect.

When Mills arrived in China, the nation's days of peace

were already numbered. There was an abortive Japanese attack that year, followed by five years of increasing tension before the real war began. With his knowledge of South China geography and the language, with his hatred of brutality and totalitarianism, his compassion for those in trouble, it was natural that Mills soon found himself detached from his mission and engaged in various war-relief activities.

It was thus that he arrived in Toishan at the time of the great famine of 1942, his job to direct various relief activities of the Canadian Red Cross. As village after village was hit by the famine, children were left behind, children who had somehow survived while their parents starved. They wandered the countryside in gangs, scavenging, stealing.

Although he had no funds or authority to go into child welfare work, Mills began to gather up the wandering waifs. He found several abandoned warehouses and was in business.

The matter of housing was comparatively easy in an area where a large proportion of the population had died, but the matter of food was not. Most of the children were ill, their bellies bloated from starvation and parasites. There were no green vegetables available, no possibility of a balanced diet. But with the help of Father O'Niel, Maryknoll priest in Toishan, Verent Mills began to solve his problems.

He does not remember who suggested pine-needle soup as a source of vitamin C. But soon Mills' waifs were having pine-needle soup once a week and the widespread signs of scurvy began to disappear.

Another serious problem remained. The children had existed as scavengers, had fed from every conceivable source, including garbage dumps. With the little food they had found, they had taken in parasites—worms. The children were filled with worms—round worms, long worms, pin worms, tape worms. Mills had neither santonin nor calomel for treatment.

One day in a casual conversation Father O'Niel mentioned that in the Philippines the people collected an herb called chenopodium. Cooked either with pork or fish, and taken once a week, it killed parasites.

"The Philippines are less than five hundred miles away. Our climate is similar. Surely it must grow here too," said Mills.

In the following days Mills and Father O'Niel scouted the local Chinese herb stores, hoping to find chenopodium oil. But there was none to be found.

In times of war and famine a missionary often develops strange contacts. So it was with Mills, who had need now and then to do business with Chinese guerrillas. This small point is not a part of the story but bears passing mention: Mills' guerrilla contacts were so good that when the Japanese captured Canton with tons of American and Canadian Red Cross supplies, he was able to do a masterful smuggling job. From under the very nose of a huge Japanese army Mills and his guerrillas smuggled a hundred tons of Red Cross drugs from Canton, up the West River and into Free China. Mills traveled in and out of Canton hidden under the floorboards of a river boat.

So now Mills asked a guerrilla friend to go to Canton and secure chenopodium oil.

Two weeks later the guerrilla returned with a small bottle, the only bottle he could find. When Mills pulled the cork he was amazed at the powerful odor of the oil—and he got an idea. If the oil gave forth such a potent stench, the plant from which the oil was derived must also smell. If the orphans could be familiarized with the smell, perhaps they could be sent forth in search parties, smelling the countryside for the plant.

In the week that followed, every child in the five Toishan orphanages became very familiar with the smell of chenopodium oil. At each home the children were lined up. A toothpick smeared with the precious oil was passed down the line, each child ordered to sniff.

"We had comments galore," says Mills, "but each child knew what we were looking for—or rather, what we were smelling for!"

And so the children went forth, the smell of chenopodium fresh in their nostrils. A week later Mills heard an excited eight-year-old in his outer office. "I must see Mi Mok-si—I must talk to Pastor Mills," shouted a small voice. The boy was brought in, a little bundle wrapped in newspaper under his arm. In the bundle was a collection of leaves. And the smell was unmistakable!

The small boy had discovered the weed growing on a garbage pile outside Toishan's East Gate. Each week thereafter the orphans of Toishan went on a chenopodium-foraging expedition. Once known, the rank two- to three-foot-high plant was found in other places. An olive green with a reddish tinge, the plant is easily recognized as it matures, turning to a reddish brown color.

The chenopodium leaves were eaten as a vegetable with dried shrimp twice a week and soon vanquished the miscellaneous collection of worms carried by every child.

The discovery of the chenopodium weed in blockaded China was important. Verent Mills sent samples to the Canadian Red Cross in Chungking, to Chengtu University farther west. Soon cabled instructions came as to how seed should be gathered so that the health-saving plant could be grown in West China. At that time China was sorely pressed by Japanese armies; all supplies had to come by air over the Hump from India. A local source of chenopodium could save lives, money, invaluable space in transport planes.

And so things were going as well as could be expected for a young missionary and his large family in an area of famine. It was then that the Japanese armies began a drive into Southwest China, a drive that threatened to engulf the Toishan area. It was obvious that Mills himself must get out. Some of the older boys could escape on their own. The problem was what to do with 142 small children, boys and girls who could not seek safety by themselves.

Verent Mills decided to head for Kukong, the wartime refugee capital of Kwangtung Province, some three hundred miles away. With nine adult Chinese as helpers the strange safari started out over the mountain range that separated Toishan from the town of Shiuhing where river boats could take the party on to Kukong.

It took two weeks to cross the mountains—a hundred miles of rugged walking in the growing heat of late spring. It was during this part of the journey that Verent Mills carried four children. To this day, fourteen years after his Long March, there are great blobs of deformed tissue on his shoulders where the Chinese carrying pole bit deep into the muscle.

Many of the children were ill when the party reached the river. It was necessary to bed down in river boats, schools, and churches while the sick could recuperate. The Japanese were never far away, but Shiuhing seemed safe. The Shiuhing Gorge lay a few miles below the city and it was unlikely that any army would attempt passage of the gorge.

Somehow the Japanese had slipped through the gorge and were within a few miles of the town. One hundred and forty-two children were awakened as shells crashed into the town, and thirty minutes later 142 uncomplaining children, each with a tiny knapsack, started out again. It was necessary again to cross mountains, to somehow flank the advancing Japanese and reach another branch of the river that would eventually lead to safety in Free China.

There were many other delays before Mills reached Kukong. By river the party finally reached the city of Kwaiping in Kwangsi Province. From Kwaiping it was another long jaunt by river to Kweilin, American air-force base in the heart of Southwest China. Then they went on by train, traveling only at night, in a circuitous route that ended at Kukong.

In Kukong many of the children were placed in the orphanage which Calvitt and Helen Clarke had taken on with the $700 raised by their first mimeographed appeal. This was Verent Mills' first and indirect contact with Calvitt Clarke.

At the end of the war Mills made what he considers the most important decision of his life. He had gone to China to become an evangelistic missionary. To thousands of Chinese he was known as Mi Mok-si, the Bulldozer Preacher. He was, and is, handy with machinery, having already begun his engineering training before going to China. In relief work he had used bulldozers, and he found that a bulldozer in the back country of China attracted a crowd just as would an elephant in the Tennessee mountains. Mills developed an effective technique. He would shuttle his 'dozer back and forth with a great noise and show of activity. As soon as a sufficient crowd had gathered, Mills would mount his mechanical charger, stop the motor, and preach.

He had gone to China to preach, he loved to preach, and he was successful. But after talking with Calvitt Clarke for five minutes in Canton in 1945, he was offered the job of running CCF's Chinese orphanages.

The war had opened Verent Mills' eyes to a whole new area of service. For three years he had lived with, and worked with, orphaned children. The Long March from Toishan had in itself been a deep, religious experience. He asked Clarke for time to consider, conferred with his mission board, took the job.

Just as the world's needy children have kept Calvitt Clarke from ever getting the pastorate he was trained for, they changed Mills' life. He is still Mi Mok-si to the hundreds of thousands of refugees in Hong Kong. He still preaches whenever he can. But Verent Mills' life for the past decade and more has been devoted to children, first China's children, later the children of the world.

By 1949, when the Communists took over China, China's Children's Fund had forty-five orphanages valued at a million dollars and caring for 5,113 children. The loss of China in 1949 ended all CCF work there and forced Mills and his wife to move once again in the face of an enemy. CCF headquarters was in Shanghai, and after months of waiting the Mills were allowed to leave. But this time it was not possible to take the children. A few have escaped. Verent Mills knows of eighty now in Hong Kong, and some of these are from the 142 who took the Long March. Fourteen boys are now teaching and preaching in Hong Kong.

CCF headquarters was re-established in Hong Kong. And as CCF began to extend its work to other countries, Hong Kong became worldwide headquarters with Verent Mills as Overseas Director.

The story of Hong Kong can be told in part by statistics, in part by specific stories.

The figures: From a population of 400,000 before China went communist the city has grown to 2,400,000. The additional 2,000,000 are refugees. There are three thousand children in Hong Kong orphanages. Seven thousand more exist as street urchins, or precariously supported by an aunt or an uncle. These seven thousand should be receiving institutional care. There are dozens of institutions in Hong Kong, including some of the largest in the world.

Three thousand children in institutions may not, at first glance, seem a large figure. But in my home state of Tennessee, with a population of nearly three and a half million, there are twenty-eight registered orphan homes with 2,318 children. More than half of the children are not orphans but are in institutions because of broken homes, a parent in prison, or because their parents are indigent. And Tennessee ranked forty-first in per capita annual income in the United States in 1953. There would presumably be a far smaller number of children in institutions in states with a higher standard of living.

The story of Hong Kong is told every day in the newspapers, in the never-ceasing accounts of boys and girls brought before the juvenile courts, the accounts of petty larceny, pickpocketing, breaking and entering.

But the story of Hong Kong and of China's children is best told through the stories of individual boys and girls in the orphanages.

Chan Kak Shing is a bright and attractive boy now in the CCF Agricultural Settlement in Hong Kong. This is his story.

"My father owned a little land and a shop in the Poo Yue district of South China. Shortly after the communists came into power he was arrested. They released him on the payment of heavy back 'taxes.' Then he was arrested again and again, and released when he paid more taxes.

"Then they did the same thing again. He could not pay any more, so they seized his shop and our little farm and kept him in prison. He hanged himself in prison, using strips of bedding and blankets which mother had taken to prison for him.

"My mother died of shock soon after Father's death. I was able to escape to Hong Kong."

Kak Shing is now eleven years old; the events he describes took place when he was only seven. But the memory of horror is still fresh; he broke down several times while telling the story.

Keung Yan Yiu's story is short. He is fourteen years old now and can give his account without tears.

"My father was a wine merchant and also owned land. He tried to co-operate with the new government. But when the persecution began he tried to escape in a junk. The communists chased the junk and sank it. Mother was with him. They both drowned. My brother and I had been left with my uncle in Canton. He paid some people to smuggle us across the border to Hong Kong. Later he got out himself but without any money. He is now a street hawker. We lived with my aunt for a while, but they are very poor. Finally we were brought to the CCF Agricultural Settlement."

Chan Kwok To now lives in the Wai Kwang Children's

Home. His official record lists him as "Adoption number WK44, Home Number CG44." But behind this bare listing is another typical story of what has happened to China's children.

"Mother died when I was very young. Father was Postmaster of the Saam Fow District in Kwangtung Province. He had taken part in the Kuomintang Government's Youth Group anti-communist activities.

"The communists arrested him as soon as they came to our district. They claimed that stamps were missing from his post office. He was thrown into prison and tortured to confess. I never saw him again, and I have no idea whether he is dead or alive."

Chui Wai-ching is a girl of fifteen, now living in the Wai Kwang Children's Home. Her father also was a "reactionary official."

Wai-ching told her story with considerable emotion.

"Father was the Magistrate, the President of the City Council and the principal of the Middle School in Ho Yuen [near Canton]. He was a popular and respected man.

"The communists arrested him, took everything from him and then turned him out penniless. All of us—relatives, friends and neighbors—were warned that if we should feed, clothe or shelter him, we would be considered traitors to the state. He died of starvation.

"Mother brought me across the border in 1950. Then she went back to Canton to get my brothers and sisters. I have not heard from her since."

Wai-ching was cared for by desperately poor refugee relatives until the burden was too great. Then she was brought to CCF.

Tsei Tzion Lung's father was a relatively high Nationalist official in Southwest China. As Chief of Police of the important city of Kweilin, it was a foregone conclusion that he would have trouble.

Young Tsei (now fourteen years old), his mother and sister were sent out across the border by one route while the father attempted to escape via Macao, the Portuguese colony forty miles from Hong Kong.

"Communist agents caught up with Father in Macao," reports Tsei Tzion Lung. "They got him through some false friends. He was drugged at a party and dragged over the border into Red China. The newspapers later published news of his execution. Mother had no money and had to give us up."

The most vivid and tragic account I heard came from sixteen-year-old Chan Kin Mun who is almost ready to graduate from the Faith-Love Home. Her father, Chan Kwok Ping, was among China's leading civilian pilots, flying military and civilian transport planes in China during and after the war.

"There were three sons and three daughters in our family," Kin Mun told me. "Mother died and Father gave up flying so that he could live with us in Canton. He was a fine writer and secured a position as correspondent for a Hong Kong newspaper, the *Wah Kiu Yat Po*. [This is the leading anti-communist Chinese language newspaper in Hong Kong.]

"We knew that Father was a marked man when the communists took over in 1949. But for a while they did not bother him. In November, 1950, in the dead of night, soldiers came banging on our door. When Father did not get to the door quickly enough, they broke it down. He was not allowed to take anything with him.

"For several weeks we took rice and other food to the

prison and sometimes were permitted to visit Father. One morning we older children left for the prison as usual. When we got there the warden told us he had left. We ran home, hoping to find him there. Then a neighbor told us that the radio had just announced that many enemies of the state were to be executed that afternoon. The names were given and Father's was on the list.

"All of us ran to Lau Fa K'iu, the big execution place in Canton. When we reached the execution grounds there were thousands of people milling around. The firing squad had already finished the job. Many bodies lay on the ground with their hands tied behind their backs.

"We managed to push through the crowd, holding hands . . . and we found him. They had shot him in the head and blown off one side of his face. I think he was still alive and knew that we were there.

"We waited until Daddy was buried with the rest of the people in a shallow mass grave. Then we went back to our home. But we had no money, and the landlord was also afraid that if he let us stay he might get into trouble. So we went to the pastor of our church and he took us in.

"It was impossible for the pastor to keep six of us indefinitely, as he was a poor man. And the police kept questioning him because of us. My oldest brother and sister finally found jobs, and another brother was taken into the home of friends.

"Some of Father's old friends smuggled three of us across the border to Hong Kong. My little brother is in this Home with me. Another brother has been adopted by a Christian family here."

And thus ended the family life of Chan Kwok Ping, airline pilot, respected writer and citizen of China.

There are hundreds of children among Hong Kong's

two million refugees who have had experiences like that of the Chan children.

CCF is spending more money on children than the British Colonial Government. Co-operating with the Church of England, the Salvation Army, the Christian Missionary Alliance, the London Mission, the Assemblies of God and *Christian Herald* magazine, CCF is supporting wholly or in part 2,300 of the colony's 3,000 institutionalized children.

The children have been scattered in a dozen small homes throughout Kowloon and the New Territories (the mainland part of Hong Kong, across the bay from the island which is the administrative center of the colony). Some of the homes are within a few hundred yards of the Red China border.

In June, 1956, CCF broke ground for the first sixty-five units of one of the most ambitious child welfare projects in the world. Children's Gardens, it is called, the tremendous new child welfare center built on the shores of a lovely bay thirty minutes by road and another thirty minutes by water from Hong Kong.

The sixty-five cottages will house a thousand children, fifteen to twenty children in each cottage with a house mother. When other units are completed in 1957 there will be schools, playgrounds, a child welfare training center.

Children's Gardens is certainly the largest Protestant orphanage in the world, perhaps *the* largest institution of its kind. Its influence will be felt far beyond the borders of one small British colony. CCF plans to use Children's Gardens as a training center for welfare workers from all over Asia. They can come to study how a modern cottage-plan orphanage operates, to study the latest methods and knowledge of child welfare work.

And even in British-owned Hong Kong there is a tremendous need for knowledge, for more modern and humane treatment of underprivileged children. The British have done a magnificent job in their refugee-swollen city. Thousands of new housing units have been built. In a city where there is no level ground this has been a difficult job, necessitating the cutting off of mountain tops so that houses and apartments can be built. But in 1956 Hong Kong still had no basic child welfare legislation, no regulations governing the treatment of children. The British governor appointed a committee headed by Verent Mills to study child welfare problems. This committee has drafted a child welfare act which probably will become the law of the colony in 1956 or 1957.

It is certainly time that Hong Kong moves into the twentieth century in this respect. In 1955 nine out of ten children admitted to institutions entered without a physical examination. In one case a child with active leprosy was admitted to a home. I saw one orphanage with two hundred children and no trained nurse. In another "orphanage" seven young orphans occupied a room with three teen-age prostitutes. In another, a retarded child was confined in a locked cage.

Most of the non-CCF homes have no recreational facilities, no books or magazines, not even a local newspaper for the children to read. And as is so often the case where large numbers of Chinese live under British rule, school facilities are woefully lacking for Chinese.

The problems of China's children do not end when they finish their education at Children's Gardens, at St. Christopher's Home or Joseph Hall. For most of the children all ties with the past have been cut. Parents are gone, relatives either gone or lost somewhere in the darkness of Communist China.

The graduate orphans must have jobs, must be given assistance, courage and faith. It is not an easy matter to place children in jobs in a city already bursting with refugees, where once-wealthy men are hawking food on the streets or poling sampans in the harbor. But this problem is being tackled by CCF as it is in other countries where there are large orphan populations.

Each summer a special camp is held for all orphans who have completed middle (high) school. For two weeks the seventeen- and eighteen-year-olds study how to get along in life. This is perhaps a strange and incongruous note: Dale Carnegie's book, *How to Win Friends and Influence People,* is used as a basic text, studied by Chinese orphans so that they can get along as Chinese in British-owned Hong Kong!

A special lecture course, two hours a day, attempts to help the boys and girls learn how to sell themselves. And over and over again the orphan graduates have dinned into them a set of simple rules: Never lie, even if by telling the truth you might lose your job; never steal, never borrow from friends or employer. Any boy or girl who is short of money is urged to come and see Mr. Mills, or Bob Arculi, his assistant, for a loan. To date six children have borrowed, all have paid their debts promptly.

The direct approach learned by CCF graduates floors Hong Kong employers. The typical Chinese approach in obtaining a job is through a middleman. The middleman, who may be a relative or a family friend, goes to the prospective employer, extols the virtues of the job-seeker. And according to Chinese custom, the job-seeker must have a "guarantor"—a businessman, shopkeeper, a well-known teacher—who will guarantee to pay back whatever the job-seeker might steal.

But CCF boys and girls, generally having no relatives, nor prosperous friends who can be guarantors, must use the direct approach. And so successful has CCF's post-graduate training been that now no CCF boy is ever asked for a guarantor. The Hong Kong Spinners, one of the Far East's largest textile mills, no longer advertises for help until it has first checked on available CCF graduates. Fifty-seven orphans were working for this firm in 1956.

There are 290 orphan graduates in Hong Kong now, and all are members of an alumni association. Dues are twelve Hong Kong dollars annually, or about $2.25. The alumni meet quarterly and have set up their own welfare fund, which now has a respectable balance of $1,600 available to needy alumni who can obtain the signatures of three other alumni.

It is generally thought that orphans have an especially difficult time adjusting to life. But this has not been the case among the Chinese orphans of Hong Kong. They are welcomed by employers, who send their recruiters out to interview graduates, as large American business concerns do. The orphan in Hong Kong is a preferred employee because he is better disciplined, has learned how to co-operate with others, fits into an organization better than a boy from a normal home.

Verent Mills is most proud of this fact: Not one of CCF's graduates has ever appeared in court. For the city of Hong Kong this is an unusual record indeed. The credit for it is due not only to the job training received by CCF children. It is due also to the sensible Christian atmosphere in which the children grow up. And much of the success is due to Mr. and Mrs. Verent Mills and Mr. and Mrs. Bob Arculi. All through the year CCF graduates are frequent guests of the Mills and Arculis. There are parties, small dinners, individual conferences when problems arise. Bob Arculi is a vitally important part of this machinery which has made respectable citizens out of scores of children who normally would have ended up as thieves, pickpockets, and dope peddlers. Bob Arculi, of Chinese-Indian parentage, was once one of the best-paid newspaper correspondents in Asia. He gave up his newspaper job to become CCF Public Relations Officer in Hong Kong at one third his former salary.

How many children have been left orphaned inside Red China? A United Nations official in Hong Kong was asked this question and simply shook his head. Nationalist Chinese sources answer briefly "millions." A newly appointed CCF orphanage superintendent, recently escaped from Communist China, tells a part of the story. He says that under the "People's Relief Association" the Reds are operating orphanages by taking over the property of Christian missions. The estimated total of children in such homes is ten thousand. However, in the liquidation of capitalists, reactionaries, and landlords, hundreds of thousands of families have been broken up. The number of children orphaned as a result can only be estimated as several million. The communists do not put such children in orphanages, as they are considered to have been tainted by the sins of their fathers and mothers.

The purge orphans are placed in huge "re-education camps" where they undergo a combination of brain-washing and hard labor. And my informant added, "In a few years there will be no such term as 'orphanages' in Red China. Practically all children will be put under mass training in big camps, whether they have parents or not."

Anyone familiar with the geopolitics of Asia will wonder at the future of CCF's vast investment in China's children. Several of the CCF homes are within shouting distance of the Communist border. Children's Gardens is nearly an hour from Hong Kong, within sight of Red China's mountains. The British admit realistically that Hong Kong could be held for perhaps ten days if the communists attacked.

But Calvitt Clarke has not gone into Hong Kong with eyes closed. He believes with others that the British colony is safe until the communists plan aggression on a world-wide—or at least Asia-wide—scale. And meanwhile the work of the Christian Children's Fund helps keep alive the image of America that, in the words of Wendell Willkie, keeps the "reservoir of good feeling" filled. CCF is a constant reminder that Americans are not all corrupt, capitalistic, money-mad warmongers. It is a daily reminder to two million Chinese that there is an America other than that described in vitriolic terms by the Communist press and radio.

But both Calvitt Clarke and Verent Mills are realistic. Mills has spent much of the past decade running with his children, first from the Japanese, then from the communists. It is always possible that another unexpected move must some day be made, that once again CCF will be itself a refugee. That time it will not be possible to bring the children, for the move must be made by water. But it will be necessary to save CCF's records, records that cover adoptions and children in thirty countries, that contain the list of thousands of other children waiting for American sponsorship. And it will be necessary also to save CCF's Hong Kong staff.

In the harbor there is a small craft, a converted thirty-foot lifeboat, *The Lady Clarke* already mentioned. Her tanks are always kept filled; she has been tested against the high seas of Lyeemun Pass which leads from the open seas to the quiet waters of the inner harbor. I have sailed in *The Lady Clarke* from her quiet anchorage in front of the Kowloon ferry slip, out through the harbor to Junk Bay. She is a small ship, to be sure; but she is seaworthy and her filled tanks will take her either to the Philippines or to Formosa if the need arises.

There is a truck parked at the Mills' home, ready for the dash to the office at 664 Nathan Road, then on to the harbor. And it is not surprising that Mi Mok-si, the Bulldozer preacher, is also a qualified navigator!

4

Children of Darkness

THIS is the story of Yasuko, as given to me by the super-intendent of a children's home in Saitami Prefecture, Japan.

"She came to us in 1946 when hundreds of children could be seen wandering in the parks and other public places. Some were older, able to fend for themselves. Others were little ones who had perhaps gotten away from their parents during the excitement of an air raid. Or perhaps the parents, no longer able to feed them, had given them away or simply sent them into the streets.

"Our policeman brought her to us. When I asked her name she slapped me in the face, cursed me. We looked at her teeth and judged that she was about six years old. But her face was older, much older.

"After she joined our home, nothing was safe. Not only did she steal constantly, but she would not eat with the other children, would not speak or play.

"After she had been with us a few days I was awakened by a noise at night. We had used the fire the evening before to boil a kettle of potatoes. It was one o'clock, the potatoes were cold. And sitting cross-legged on the kitchen table was our girl, eating cold potatoes. Hungrily she stuffed them into her mouth. 'Are you hungry?' I asked. There was no answer.

"During the days that followed there was no response, no co-operation whatsoever. Never could we get a word about her past, names of places or people—just a frightened sideways glance, the form of a little girl turned away with fear written on her face. We had named her Yasuko, Child of Peace. But she became instead a child of the night.

"Every night I went to the kitchen, helping her get the food she would not eat during the day. For she had led a life of theft, stealing by day and like an animal, eating after dark. I shared her darkness in the hope that some day she might be willing to share our light.

"And it worked. On the tenth night she spoke to me, told me that I would no longer have to join her in the darkness. She would eat now with the others. She began to speak; but we felt that it was almost easier to deal with her when she did not talk; for her language was not the language of decent people.

"It was a hard struggle. But it was victorious. Yasuko is sixteen now. Her good grades have won her a scholarship in senior high school. She is a fine girl whom we can trust in every respect. The fright and sadness in her eyes are gone now, replaced with a merry twinkle. She has many friends among the other girls. And of all the children here, it is Yasuko who shows the deepest affection and tenderness. Our child of the night has indeed become a child of peace."

There are many other children of modern Japan who have lived in the shadows caused by war as Yasuko has. There is the story of Etsuo, whose name means Child of Joy.

In 1945 Etsuo's father, Tateo, was the owner of a prosperous restaurant in a Tokyo industrial area. Tateo had four children by his wife and two children by one of his waitresses. He was able to support this double family because the restaurant was near a railroad station and was well patronized.

Near the end of the war Tateo's business establishment and home were destroyed during an American air raid. He sent his legal wife, who was now pregnant again, to a village in the country. He took his mistress and her two boys to another country village and began a new life peddling fish.

Etsuo, Child of Joy, was born to the legal wife in 1946. His father had now abandoned the family, and when Etsuo was four his mother died of malnutrition. The children were divided among relatives, and it was Etsuo's lot to be sent back to his father. Meanwhile Tateo had still another child, a girl, by his mistress. He now had a family of six to feed. To make ends meet his mistress obtained a job as a waitress in another prefecture while Tateo continued to peddle fish. For nearly a year the mistress sent money each month. Then she disappeared, leaving Tateo with four children.

As the family fortunes deteriorated, Etsuo's lot became more and more difficult. His father went to work before daylight, leaving Etsuo to the not-too-tender mercies of his half-brothers and half-sister. The little boy was systematically starved, frequently beaten. In desperation he began to steal food from neighbors.

The father, returning home at night, would hear the neighbors' complaints about stolen food. Not believing the little boy's story of being starved and mistreated by the older children, Tateo began to give Etsuo daily beatings.

Thus for Etsuo, Child of Joy, each day was a repetition of hunger, stealing, beatings. In April, 1951, Tateo decided to punish the boy in a new manner. He set fire to clumps of moxa grass and held the burning grass against the little boy's body.

Soon Etsuo's body was covered with burns. Hating his half-brothers and -sister, fearing his father, he began to run away, finding shelter wherever he could. The neighbors would report the boy's whereabouts; Tateo would bring him home—and more moxa grass would be burned against his body. His legs were a mass of scars, his body bloated from starvation. But in December, 1951, he had the strength to run away again, this time disappearing for a week.

On the eighth day Etsuo was discovered sleeping among the rocks on the outskirts of a village several miles from his home. Again his father was summoned. But this time there was no more burning, no beating. Even the father could see that there was something seriously wrong with the boy. His toes and feet were black and swollen. Neighbors insisted that a doctor be called.

Etsuo's trouble was quickly diagnosed as frostbite. After a week spent in the December snow, the frostbite had progressed to a point where gangrene was inevitable. It was necessary to amputate one leg and all of the toes on the other foot.

The little boy's plight received wide attention. The father was arrested for cruelty, the people of the prefecture showered Etsuo with toys. In April, 1952, the Child of Joy was placed in an orphanage operated by the Lutheran Church. He has become expert with crutches, does well in school, although several years behind children of his age. Through the Christian Children's Fund he now has an American family.

Etsuo's story is typical of many children in the orphanages of Japan. His plight is an indirect result of war, of the cruelty, immorality and complicated family situations that have come frequently in war's aftermath.

The record does not indicate whether Akikuni's father died directly or indirectly as a result of the war. After the father died in April, 1944, Aki and his mother became wanderers and beggars. In July, 1949, they arrived in Osaka. The mother soon remarried, and Aki began to go to school.

But Aki's stepfather mistreated him badly, and he began the first of many attempts to run away from home. The years 1950 through 1952 were a repetition of escapes, of days wandering and begging, of being found by the police and taken home again. In late 1952 Aki's mother left his stepfather, and the two began to wander together. By day they begged in a park; by night they slept in subway entrances. As the boy grew older he began to operate on his own. From time to time he was picked up by the police, placed in a child welfare shelter or home. But he had by now become adept at escape.

In June, 1953, Aki was caught by police stealing twenty-eight yen (about eight cents) from the offering box of a Buddhist shrine. Soon afterward he was brought to a home affiliated with CCF. The mother meanwhile had disappeared, and the stepfather had been convicted of stealing.

It would be only natural that Aki, eleven years old when he was placed in the Home, would continue his attempts at escape. Most of his life had been spent as a vagrant; he had learned to beg and steal, liked the life he led because he could remember no other.

During the first year Aki ran away several times, returning to his old haunts in Osaka's Tennoji Park. One of the instructors in the Children's Home who had taken special interest in the boy would follow and find him. An unhappy Aki would be brought back, his heart filled with rebellion and hate.

Aki is now fourteen years old. Kind treatment, the unfailing interest of the instructor, have finally washed away the rebellion. He now has many friends among the other boys, has not attempted an escape since April, 1955. Aki, the vagrant beggar boy, may be well on the way to complete rehabilitation.

In visiting homes affiliated with the Christian Children's Fund I heard scores of similar stories. There is twelve-year-old Shizuki, brought to the Yokushima Fujin Home in 1947 by a welfare worker. She had been found living in the bell tower of a temple, cared for by a thirteen-year-old sister. Shizuki's skin was the color of dirt, she weighed ten pounds at the age of three.

"We could hold her in one hand," the superintendent recalls. "I still feel a coldness within me when I remember her story. When we put her on quilts to sleep she would cry and cry. Then she would roll over until she came to the cold boards. Only then could she sleep. We all wondered what could be done with Shizuki. It was difficult, but now she is a healthy girl, with a cheerful personality. We wonder if she has any memories of life in the bell tower."

The Japanese Government is the only government in Asia that has accurate statistics by which the social problems of its people can be measured. The last complete report of the Children's Bureau, Ministry of Health and Welfare, made in mid-1953, gives these revealing statistics on the children of post-war Japan:

Mentally ill	78,300
Blind	16,200

Deaf and dumb	27,700
Physically handicapped	129,200
Physically weak	98,100
Delinquent	41,100
Lacking proper care	260,600
Lacking in proper guardianship (generally orphans or half-orphans)	92,400

The total, 743,600, represents nine per cent of the total population of Japan. These are children not receiving the help they need. This figure does not include 45,000 children in various types of private and public homes for orphans, the blind, the physically and mentally handicapped.

In late 1955 the Ministry of Health and Welfare announced that based upon nationwide samplings there were 98,000 children in Japan who should either be in children's homes or have foster parents. And in 1956, Seiji Giga, Director of Christian Children's Fund operations in Japan, made an independent study indicating there were 30,000 children who qualified for care in orphanages.

These statistics are startling when we consider that Japan enjoys economic stability and good government that is the exception rather than the rule in Asia. It has been eleven years since the last of World War II bombings, which means that a large number of Japan's orphans are not war orphans. Only those eleven years or older could have lost their parents during the war. Perhaps these figures are in large measure a result of the governmental structure of Japan which traditionally has reached into every home, making accurate statistics possible. Perhaps also the fact that Japan is one of the few nations in the Far

East with a basic child welfare law, with well-staffed social services, enters into the picture.

One other statistic is of importance. The 1953 report of the Children's Bureau listed 8,722 child welfare institutions of all types. Of these, 502 are children's homes of which 109 are maintained by various levels of the Japanese Government and 343 by private organizations. There are 30,124 children in the institutions, giving Japan a larger number of children receiving institutional care than any other country in Asia except Korea.

If the figures are accurate, and there would be no reason for the government to exaggerate its child welfare problems, we can imagine what similar statistics on other countries in Asia would reveal—nations such as Korea and India.

The stories of Etsuo, Yasuko, Aki, and Shizuki typify those of the hundreds of children I met in the children's homes of Japan. Many have been orphaned as a direct result of war; many more as an indirect result. In spite of apparent stability, there are still numerous beggars and their children. Hundreds of young girls are sold into prostitution by their own families. There are children who become institutionalized because of the tensions that break up families, who are viciously mistreated by step-parents unable properly to take the place of parents killed during the bombings.

Japan fortunately has a child welfare act, called the Children's Charter, and is doing more for its needy children than any other nation in the Far East. The Children's Bureau is staffed by well-trained workers, and Japan's tight and efficient governmental system makes it possible to locate abandoned children and get them into institutions. The days of children living in bell towers are over, but an enormous problem remains.

In Japan the Christian Children's Fund is helping to support more children in more homes than in any other country except Korea. In 1956, 2,315 children were receiving assistance in forty-two homes. One home in the southern island of Kyushu is entirely CCF supported. In April, 1956, the six cottages of the model Bott Memorial Home in Tokyo were completed, and when the rest of the facilities are finished in late 1956 this CCF-built home will become Japan's model child welfare institution.

But for the most part CCF gives assistance to established Protestant Homes. The Japanese Government gives a grant to every needy child, but the help lacks a great deal of paying for the child's care. The deficit must be made up by local church groups, by organizations like CCF and, in the Tokyo area, by gifts from Americans. With aid from these sources and with the help of well-trained staffs, the homes in Japan are certainly the best in Asia.

Tokyo Ikusei-en is an example of the best among Japan's children's homes. The home was established by Mrs. Hatsu Kitagawa in 1896 to take care of twenty-six children who lost their parents in a giant tidal wave that struck the northeastern coast of Japan. After Mrs. Kitagawa's death in 1932, Masanori Matsushima became superintendent; and his success is indicated by the testimonials from government officials that crowd the walls of his office.

There is a small swimming pool at the Tokyo Ikusei-en. A professionally trained child psychologist comes to the home twice weekly. There is a child guidance clinic for mothers, and a special mothers' library. Thus the home serves the whole community. I found this the pattern at other homes. Not only are orphaned children given excellent care. The homes serve as training centers for hundreds of mothers in the community, giving them access to professional services and libraries helpful in solving their own problems.

Mr. Matsushima, like the other superintendents, is a man of considerable training and competence. But ingenuity in addition to training is often necessary to care for children in crowded quarters. At his home, Mr. Matsushima has solved the problem of combined sleeping and living quarters in a unique manner. He has designed a special roll-into-the-wall bed, a deep drawer about five feet long which is pulled out at night and serves as a bed. During the day the beds are pushed back into the wall makng the whole room available for play and study.

In other homes I noted another example of ingenuity. Everywhere there were animals—mice, rats, chickens, dogs. In some homes every child has his pet even if it be merely a white mouse in a cage. The Japanese have found that if children are given animals, they have an opportunity to compensate for lost love and security. They lavish love and care on their pets, and in every home where animals have been added the children have become much happier and better disciplined.

The Japanese homes, even though frequently housed in one or two large buildings, are actually run on the cottage plan. A house mother cares for from fifteen to twenty-five children. The children thus receive considerable individual care plus the generally good welfare services provided by consultants.

CCF in Japan is a smoothly running organization, appreciated by the Japanese Government and receiving excellent co-operation from it. Much of its success is due to Seiji Giga, CCF's Executive Director. Giga is a trained welfare worker with several years experience in juvenile delinquency. After the war he was a welfare worker with the Army of Occupation. He runs his office with two assistants, handling some one thousand letters between children and their sponsors plus between three and four hundred gift packages a year.

Giga was five years out of college when Japan attacked Pearl Harbor. He was not distinguished as a supporter of the war, spent some difficult periods in jail because of his courage in criticizing his government. He is one of the best-balanced young Japanese I have ever met, sensibly critical of America but also pro-American. He is also highly competent in his chosen field.

Seiji Giga is convinced that the work of CCF and similar organizations is extremely worth while, provided there is constant follow-up and tight organization. He pointed out that Norman Cousins had attempted to develop a "foster parent" plan for victims of Hiroshima. But sponsors lost interest because of poor follow-up, the lack of an organization to keep a flow of correspondence going between child and sponsor. Giga also points out one inevitable human problem of a widespread sponsorship program.

In every Japanese home, he finds, there are two or three children who receive many letters and packages each year. There are other sponsored children who receive only occasional letters or remembrances; and there are those who receive nothing but financial help.

The difference in interest of different sponsors causes jealousies among the children. The child who receives no letters naturally wonders why another child should be deluged with mail and gifts. The unsponsored child, receiving no letters and no financial help either, can become embittered. But Giga sees this problem as a challenge. It is a challenge to the personnel of the homes, who can use the disparity in sponsors' generosity to develop habits of sharing among the children. It is also a challenge to America to give more help to the children of their enemy of a decade ago.

Many Americans in Japan have met this challenge. There are gifts from enlisted men, from clubs, from the wives of officers and men. There have been a few Americans like Ambassador Joseph Grew, once interned by the Japanese, who gave one million yen to a Japanese orphanage. This money, nearly $3,000, came from the royalties on Mr. Grew's autobiography.

Unfortunately we in America have been slow to give help to the children of Japan. There are understandable prejudices, perhaps, held by most of us in some degree. But if our government can accept Japan as a reliable ally we should be able to accept the Japanese as friends.

In the forty-two CCF affiliated orphanages there are six hundred unsponsored children. There are an additional twenty-five Protestant-supported orphanages with hundreds of children needing the money and the warmth a sponsor can provide. The war orphans, the children of the bombings, are moving out. But there are more children moving in, in need of help. In two typical homes I found that only twenty-seven and eleven out of ninety-seven and fifty-five children were war orphans.

The others are the new crop of children. Seiji Giga believes there are a minimum of thirty thousand who should be receiving the kind of care that made Yasuko, Child of the Night, into a child of peace.

5

The Shrimps Get Hurt

"WHEN the whales fight, the shrimps get hurt"—so goes a Korean proverb that comes true in the blighted lives of Korea's children, caught by the thousands in the aftermath of war.

The plight of Korea's children, at least, has been well publicized. In late 1956 Universal-International Pictures will release the film *Battle Hymn* which tells the story of Colonel Dean Hess who in 1951 led a group of American and Korean pilots in the evacuation of nearly one thousand orphans from Seoul to the safety of Cheju Island.

During the fighting, and with less frequency after the truce, there were a succession of stories about Korean orphans. There were numerous incidents of American soldiers establishing small orphanages on their own initiative, of individual children being legally adopted. Even in 1955 and 1956 the accounts continue, stories such as that of Harry Holt, a fifty-year-old Oregon farmer with the self-imposed mission of finding homes for all the GI babies in Korea. In early 1956 Mr. Holt announced that he intended to place at least five hundred Korean mixed-bloods before the year was over. Through an organization known as World Vision, Inc., the Holts are themselves supporting thirty-three orphans at a total cost of $330 a month.

But in spite of the Holts and many like them, the need is still immense. Unlike Japan, there are no accurate figures available on the number of children still wandering the streets of Korea, on those in private homes who need assistance. The Korean Social Welfare Ministry estimates there are only five thousand children on the streets. Much more accurate is the figure of an organization whose name can best be translated as "The National Vagabonds Guilding Association." The Vagabonds estimate a total of 167,-000 homeless persons, of whom 40,000 are children. In Seoul alone the Vagabonds count 2,471 delinquent boys, with girls not mentioned.

The Korean Government is able to give accurate figures on the number of orphanages and children in institutions. In 1956 there were 474 registered homes housing 50,045 children. There are some of the best orphanages in the world in Korea, also some of the worst. There are tiny homes, housing a handful of children, supported by a minister or an American GI. There are enormous institutions like Mrs. O. S. Whang's home on Cheju Island, caring for one thousand children, 550 of them supported by CCF.

There is little one can write of the children of Korea that has not been written. I was in Seoul in June, 1950, when the communists struck south across the 38th parallel. On the war's second day I visited the railroad station, saw the first numb and bewildered refugees arrive. And I have been back three times since, have seen the ragged hordes of street urchins that wander the streets of every city.

I once made a count of children seen during a fifteen-minute walk in refugee-swollen Pusan. There were forty-four street children lying uncared for on the sidewalk or in the gutter, fourteen of them desperately ill. It is in Pusan and the other cities far behind the fighting lines of 1950-53 that one sees the most concentrated misery.

Many of the "shrimps" die during the cold nights of the Korean winter. The more hardy somehow survive, managing to steal sufficient food, to find places to sleep at night. As these children grow older they concentrate in gangs, learning from one another new methods of stealing and pilfering. Hundreds become junior pimps or join the gangs that break into U.S. Army storehouses and freight cars. Every black market gang has its orphan break-in specialists.

The less daring children survive by begging, by setting up shoeshine operations on the city streets, or by less ambitious excursions into larceny. It is not safe now to walk down the streets of Seoul with a fountain pen showing, for there must be one gang that has specialized in training children in the art of snatching a pen or pencil from an outside pocket, then melting into the crowds that always jam the city. There are also the hat-snatchers, specializing in removing foreigners' hats with a sleight-of-hand technique so quick that it defies detection.

There is the story of an American Army jeep, en route across Seoul with a bag full of local currency, the payroll for the Korean employees of an army unit. The vehicle did not stop, the money bag was guarded by one of the American soldiers. Yet when the soldiers arrived at their destination, the money had disappeared.

More than in any nation in the world, children in Korea are being molded into criminals, into juvenile delinquents who are rapidly becoming crafty adult crooks. For the girls who survive, the solution is obvious: prostitution. A recent estimate of one prostitute out of every eight females in the Seoul area indicates the nature of this problem.

Certainly Americans have opened their hearts to the children of Korea. Hundreds of men, like Colonel Hess, have done their part in saving children who would otherwise be lost. Hundreds of children have become mascots of U.S. Army units, to be cared for, spoiled. One of the problems in Korea today is that the American soldiers are leaving. The boy who became a pampered mascot is left behind, more American than Korean, to face the problem of living as a Korean again.

There is still another problem in connection with the American soldier who has done so much to help the children of Korea. As the months pass, men stationed in Korea become more and more embittered at their lot, less interested in helping Koreans. Where two or three years ago stories of Americans establishing orphanages, adopting children, even building schools, were commonplace, such stories now are much less frequent.

An Eighth Army public relations officer told me in 1955 that it is frequently necessary now to improvise or to actually invent a good-deed story. We can hardly blame the young GI, who is stationed along the demilitarized line in what must seem to him a senseless waste of his youth. The Koreans themselves, driven and harried by inflation, by an uncertain future, frequently make themselves disliked and hated.

Thus, Korea in 1956, three years after the signing of the truce, still faces the most pressing social problems of any nation in Asia. Problems are increasing because so many of those who helped are gone or are unwilling to give more assistance.

The Korean Government attempts to solve its problems. It grants, for instance, five whan per month for every child in an institution. But as one orphanage superintendent said to me, "That is not even enough to buy the sugar to put in a cup of coffee!"

Five whan is equivalent to a varying fraction of one U.S. cent. The currency fluctuates violently, especially around U.S. Army paydays. For immediately afterward, the black market is flooded with American Army scrip as the GI's wheel and deal for women and commodities. In general the value of five whan can be figured at between a half cent and one cent.

The Korean Government also from time to time attempts to clear children from the streets. A police or army truck goes forth; all the ragged children in sight are corralled and taken away somewhere.

Dr. K. S. Oh, Superintendent of CCF's model cottage orphanage at Anyang, told me of a typical day in 1955. The temperature hovered at zero when an Army truck drove up to the home with fifty shivering children. The Anyang Home has a normal population of 205 children; it was impossible to house fifty additional children, with or without warning. Dr. Oh took in fifteen of the smallest waifs. The remainder of this pitiful cargo was undoubtedly dumped somewhere else down the road.

The children who have survived, who now live by their wits, do not take well to confinement. Inevitably those who are picked up in the dragnet and unceremoniously dumped in an orphanage attempt to escape. And it is obviously impossible to know the case histories of those who thus become institutionalized. The smaller ones remember only dimly a battle or a bombing back in 1950 or 1951, remember finding themselves homeless, joining a white-clad throng of refugees moving southward. There are hundreds of five- to eight-year-olds in Korea who have no idea where they were born, what village they once called home, what their fathers did for a living.

The responsibility of caring for its homeless children is beyond the capacity of the Korean Government. In Japan it is possible to spend 11 per cent of the national budget on welfare services. But Korea, with one fourth the population of Japan, has armed forces five times as large. It is even necessary, or so the Korean Government believes, to tax its children's homes. In 1955 the Christian Children's Home at Anyang paid a whopping 450,000-whan tax bill.

Numerous American organizations are at work in Korea, helping to solve this problem of mass want and delinquency. The Save the Children Federation, with headquarters in New York, is helping 1,700 children in private homes, has sponsored twenty-one schools, has developed community projects of the 4-H type for rural children. Evangelist Bob Pierce through his World Vision, Inc., is supporting orphans in numerous homes. Five American Protestant denominations are at work in the field, the main attack being made by the Methodists and the Presbyterians.

And the Christian Children's Fund probably spends more money on Korea's children than all the rest combined. In 1956 CCF budgeted $656,000 for its Korean operations, including sponsorship of 9,728 children in seventy-two orphanages. An operation of this magnitude requires a local organization of some size, a competent local executive committee. The program is supervised by Ernest Nash, who spent many years in Shanghai as Deputy Chief of the city's international concession government.

In Korea it is necessary not only to take in needy children. There is a tremendous need to train welfare workers, to develop minimum standards of operation in the myriad homes that dot the land. There is also a problem of mixed-blood children, though not as big as one would expect considering the scores of thousands of American and Allied troops stationed in Korea since 1950. It is estimated that there are approximately one thousand mixed-blood children.

The CCF Korea program is fortunate in having the benefit of a trained child welfare worker. The Mennonite Church's Central Committee has assigned Miss Helen Tieszen to CCF on a permanent-loan basis. With the financial co-operation of the American-Korean Foundation she has established training classes for orphanage personnel in all sections of South Korea.

In Korea there are special child welfare problems, found only in a nation subjected to intense warfare for three years. Among the country's 22,000 amputee cases, many are children. There are numerous children blinded as a result of bombings. There is inevitably a high incidence of TB.

American organizations have attacked all these problems, and CCF has done its share among the blind and tubercular, operating a Health Home for the latter group at Pusan and four homes for blind children.

Even among the CCF-affiliated homes there are some that are poorly administered because there are an insufficient number of people in Korea trained to do an efficient job. But there are also outstanding institutions, including some of the finest in the world. The Christian Children's Home at Anyang is one of these, the first cottage-plan orphanage built in Asia. Supervised by eighty-two-year-old Dr. K. S. Oh, graduate of the University of Louisville and dean of Korean physicians, the home at Anyang shows what can be done when funds and trained personnel are available.

Dr. Oh has been active in children's work for many years, has seen warfare and its tragic effect on children in all its nastiness. In 1952 American planes bombed the Home by mistake. Napalm bombs were used, snuffing out the lives of eighty-six children in one spot. Clustered around the place where the children were burned to death are lovely new white cottages where fifteen children live with their house mothers. The home has its own fields, raises its own livestock, harvests chestnuts from the grove that surrounds the property. One hundred and fifty-two of the 205 children at Anyang have American sponsors. The cottages were built by CCF as one of the remarkable extras which Dr. Clarke is able to squeeze from CCF's income from sponsors.

There are a half dozen other homes, built by or wholly operated by CCF. The Nam Book Home in the outskirts of Seoul falls into this category. But Nam Book, with its 178 children and up-to-date facilities, is remarkable for another reason. It is one of several joint projects, administered by CCF but largely financed by the *Christian Herald* magazine. *Christian Herald*, the largest interdenominational religious magazine in the world, has a long history of excellent child welfare work overseas and in America. The CCF-*Christian Herald* partnership extends to five other homes in Korea, a large orphanage in Hong Kong and an excellent rural vocational home in central Formosa. It has been the co-operation of *Christian Herald*, the major Protestant denominations in Korea, and numberless American soldiers that has made it possible for CCF to assist over nine thousand children in Korea.

During the Korean war, Americans responded generously to the need. One appeal advertisement, mentioned in a previous chapter, brought in nearly $500,000 in sponsorships. But Americans seem to be front-page readers who respond best in times of great crisis. An account of a great battle, the wiping out of a city, news pictures showing thousands of refugees—these are the things that move us to giving. The problems of keeping an uneasy truce, the political goings-on in South Korea, do not touch our hearts so readily. Yet though Korea has moved off the front pages, its problems and CCF's problems continue. Not only must approximately nine thousand children in seventy-two homes be supported. Somehow help must be found for the thousands more who still need it. On January 1, 1956, a total of 120 additional children's homes in South Korea, with 12,000 children, had applied to the Christian Children's Fund for help.

American sponsors of Korean children have been generous. The Korea office of CCF handles 50,000 letters a year; last year it translated from Korean into English a total of 11,000 letters from Korean children to their American sponsors. Almost every child receives a birthday or Christmas gift, some of the gifts being unnecessarily lavish.

The problem now is to find more Americans willing to take on more children. The opportunities in Korea are limitless. CCF, Save the Children Federation, World Vision, and the Methodist, Presbyterian, Holiness and Mennonite Churches all offer channels through which Americans may give.

I have a warm spot in my heart for the Koreans; for I lived among them for three years, lost my own home and possessions when the communists crossed the 38th parallel in 1950. I have always objected to statements that

America and the United Nations won a victory in Korea; for victory or defeat must be measured in terms other than square miles of territory lost and regained. As long as there are forty thousand homeless children wandering the streets and alleys of Korea, there can be no victory in the real sense.

Many of the children are probably beyond redemption; they have learned to live by their wits and are unwilling to submit to captivity. The effects of war such as devastated Korea do not wear off quickly. But every day, somewhere in Korea, a child is picked up by a missionary, a kindly passer-by, a soldier, and can be redeemed. Such a child is An Hua-sil, of the Christian Children's Home at Anyang.

Hua-sil was picked up by Dr. Oh at the Anyang railroad station in October of 1955. Abandoned, she was skin and bones, dressed in rags. Five-year-old Hua-sil might have lasted another day or so. There was no room at the home for her, but Dr. Oh managed to make room.

I met An Hua-sil after she had been in Anyang for two months. Had I not seen the picture taken on the day of her arrival, I would not believe that such a transformation could take place. No one can know when the child was born, or through what tragedy she has lived. Probably she was born about the time Korea's war began. Were her parents living in the North, were they perhaps among the hundreds of thousands who fled southward? Was her father killed or imprisoned? Did the family spend weeks walking and running in the vanguard of advancing armies? None of these facts will ever be known. And as far as An Hua-sil is concerned, the past is unimportant. For if there be scars they are well concealed. Hua-sil now is among the happiest girls at Anyang, physically as robust as any other child in the home.

There are an even score of children at Anyang who came unknown and nameless. Wherever there has been war, in Japan, in China, in Korea, this is a frequent occurrence. Sometimes the child is given a name descriptive of his or her arrival. Thus a little boy, found abandoned under a chestnut tree at Anyang, is to this day known as "Little Chestnut." But more frequently the people of war-torn Asia show their deep longing for peace and tranquillity in the names they give their nameless waifs. An Hua-sil means "Little Flower of Peace."

6

The Overseas Chinese

THE war in Korea ended in 1953. The war in Indo-China ended in 1954. The war in the jungles of Malaya almost ended in 1955, but keeps sputtering on in occasional paroxysms of ambush and murder. For the ten million overseas Chinese in Southeast Asia, these wars are vitally significant. Even the Chinese in Singapore have a stake in happenings in Korea, four thousand miles away. The Chinese are caught in the middle of these shooting wars, in their sometimes strange economic effects. Thus the Korean war thrust the price of pepper sky high; the Chinese pepper growers were prosperous; the price of babies on the baby market hit a low.

Except in Indo-China with its 600,000 refugees, the known problems of children in Southeast Asia are largely confined to the Chinese. In part this is because centuries ago the apostles of Mohammed did a thorough missionary job in Malaya, Borneo, Indonesia. In areas under British control the right of the Malay to his faith, undisturbed, is a part of ancient treaties, made between the British and local sultans. It is almost impossible for Christian agencies to assist Moslem children who might need assistance. And very few Malays seek help. If a Malay child is taken into an orphanage the law provides that he must be provided special worship facilities, a diet in accordance with Moslem faith. Obviously this makes operation of non-Moslem homes for Malay children difficult if not impossible.

In addition, the easygoing Malay is not likely to get into trouble. It is the Chinese teenager rather than the Malay who is found in Singapore's juvenile court. It is the young Chinese who frequently becomes involved in opium smuggling, in terrorist activities.

There are unbelievably wealthy Chinese in Southeast Asia, men like George Lee of Singapore, owner of the largest Chinese-language newspaper outside China, proprietor of rubber plantations, agent for Nash cars, Frigidaire, Admiral products. At the same time there are thousands of Chinese like Wang Tak An of Borneo, a young widow dying of TB, desperately trying to find someone to adopt her baby. For she knows that in the manner of local Chinese, her relatives will sell the child into slavery after her death.

In the nations of Southeast Asia there are thirteen orphanages affiliated with the Christian Children's Fund. A total of 531 children are sponsored by Americans. In Vietnam there is a home for refugee children of the Indo-China war. In Indonesia there is a home for children of mixed Dutch-Indonesian or Chinese-Indonesian blood. In all the other eleven orphanages, except for an occasional Tamil or a child from an aboriginal mountain tribe, the children are Chinese.

The problems of children are especially acute in those parts of Southeast Asia under British control, partly because of the strange inconsistencies of British rule. Thus, in Singapore there is one of the most complete cradle-to-grave welfare programs in the world, with tremendous new low-cost housing developments and free hospitalization. Yet for a century no effort was made to provide

Chinese children with educational facilities. No effort has been made to stop the malicious practice of selling children into a life of slavery.

In Sarawak, British North Borneo, there is an excellent home for juvenile delinquents. But only those teenagers who get into trouble, who eventually appear in juvenile court, can get into the home. For the orphaned or needy young Chinese who does not get into trouble there is no place to go. Also in North Borneo it is possible to buy opium in every town. The attitude seems to be that opium has always been there, is a part of local tradition; therefore, the trade should not be curtailed.

Except for one home for blind children operated by the Church of England, all the homes of Singapore and Malaya are run by the Salvation Army. And except for one babies' home in Singapore, the homes are in ancient buildings where children are badly crowded, sleeping sometimes thirty and forty to a room. The exception is of interest, for it was made possible by the gift of a rich Chinese, brother of one of Singapore's most ardent pro-communist Chinese businessmen.

Most of the boys and girls in the homes of Malaya come from unbelievably sordid backgrounds. Typical is the story of seven-year-old Moi Suwei. After her mother died, her father married again. The stepmother murdered the father and the little girl was left with a grandmother who was a leading communist terrorist in the jungles near Ipoh.

Or there is the story of two children, a girl aged four, a boy of six. The children's mother died and the father refused to work. Until juvenile authorities placed the children in a home, they supported their father by begging among the brothels of Singapore.

At the Salvation Army Babies' Home I saw attractive little Joe Chua, found on the streets weighing thirteen pounds—at two and a half years of age. Little Joe's mother was dead, his father was an ignorant tri-shaw puller (the tri-shaw is a mechanized Malayan version of the rickshaw) and simply neglected to feed the boy. Joe Chua has regained most of his weight but because of months of starvation has not yet learned to walk.

There are untainted children of lepers, children with both parents dying of TB, children used by their parents to smuggle opium, numerous children whose mother or father, or both, have been murdered. In every home there are a few products of the jungle warfare that has now gone on for a decade, children like those of the Ong family. Their father became a communist jungle fighter, deserting the family. The mother was killed because she was not a communist sympathizer, and three children, a girl of fifteen, a boy of eight, a girl of seven, were left homeless.

The brutality of Malaya's jungle warfare has never been appreciated in America; after all, it is a small war and far away. No one knows the number of children who have been affected by it. Donald Moore, Singapore's crusading anticommunist publisher and writer, describes the jungle war in his book *We Live in Singapore*.

When they have tied a few dozen defenseless men to trees and slowly hacked them to pieces with knives; when they have flung women, screaming, into blazing smoke-houses; when they have shot children, apparently without caring; then it is difficult to resist the conclusion that you are no longer dealing with men, but with a species of wild animal. These murderers of Malaya are not misguided youths; nor are they ill-advised and foolish adults. They are loathsome, degenerate killers waging a horrible war that knows no quarter. At the same time they are heroes and objects of praise and admiration in communist countries.

The Chinese children of Malaya have been kidnaped as hostages in the jungle war. They have been frequently murdered in retaliation against men who did not sympathize, who refused to co-operate. They have been used as runners, spies, agents.

Many of the children come to the homes near death from starvation. I met a charming little six-year-old, brought to the Salvation Army Babies' Home in Singapore. When she sat down for her first meal she looked at the food, saying, "Is this whole bowl of rice for me?" Her case history is typical. She is one of four children. Her mother is in a mental hospital and her father is an opium smoker so far gone that all his money goes into the purchase of opium. No effort is made to rehabilitate such men; perhaps there are so many that rehabilitation is impossible.

In all my travels I found no place where there is more cruelty to children. Only in Korea are children found so frequently near death from starvation. And only in Singapore did I find so many small children used by their parents or by relatives to beg, particularly among the brothels; to act as juvenile pimps and procurers, as opium runners. All of the vices, the brutality, the nastiness of old China of a century ago are found among the Chinese of Singapore.

It is little wonder that Communism finds ready recruits in this cesspool of Asia. It is not entirely the fault of the Chinese. Making up eighty per cent of Singapore's population, contributing economically what the easygoing

Malay could not and perhaps never can contribute, the Chinese have been considered aliens. Until very recently their children could be educated only by going to private Chinese schools. Vicious customs long since outlawed in China were maintained because no one took the trouble to outlaw them.

In addition to the Salvation Army Homes, the Government of Singapore and of the Federated States now maintains institutions for children. In Singapore there is a special government home for juvenile prostitutes (some aged ten and eleven); a girls' craft center where two hundred girls are receiving vocational training; a home for delinquent boys. More and more it is realized that the Chinese must receive better treatment. An efficient juvenile court system is being developed so that boys and girls who can be rehabilitated are separated from the incorrigibles and sent to homes.

It is not the fault of the Salvation Army that its facilities for needy children are poor. Not a rich organization, the Army must always obtain a considerable part of its financing locally. Large capital funds are needed to repair its crumbling buildings, to build necessary new facilities. Besides, the Chinese children of Malaya need facilities which by its very nature the Salvation Army cannot provide. It is an organization run along military lines; and in a military setup there is no place for cottage-plan homes, for house mothers and individual attention. It is difficult for the warped children of Singapore's slums and Malaya's war to become mentally whole again, to achieve the security they have lost, in an atmosphere of military rigidity and crowded dormitories. They can be taught a trade, but I wonder how well they can be taught to live.

The conditions of children in Singapore are duplicated

in varying degree in all parts of Southeast Asia where there are large Chinese populations. And this means everywhere. Population figures for 1954 show 1,000,000 Chinese in Vietnam; 893,000 in Singapore; 218,000 in Cambodia; 3,500,000 in Thailand; 1,600,000 in Indonesia; 360,-000 in Burma, and 221,000 in North Borneo.

The selling of children as slaves is a part of Chinese custom in all these nations. But it was in North Borneo that I became best acquainted with this custom. The Chinese of North Borneo, and in particular of the colony of Sarawak, come largely from the part of the China coast where I lived as a child. There are many Chinese from the very town in which I was born. In the cities, even far in the jungles, I found Chinese with whom I could converse in the Foochow dialect.

Rubber and pepper are gods as powerful as the "Grandfather Idol" and the "Empty Heaven God" who have numerous temples in Sarawak. When the price of pepper and rubber is high, conditions are good and the number of children sold as slaves decreases.

The average price for children runs to $150 for girls and $100 for boys in the area of Kuching, Sarawak's capital. In Sibu the average prices are higher, but girls bring less than boys: in mid-1956 quotations there ran as high as $300 for a boy and somewhat less for a girl.

Girls are frequently purchased as "wives" for sons in the family. They are called "adopted daughters" but in reality they are slaves, nothing more. The Malays rarely sell their own children but frequently buy Chinese children, paying an average of $100 for a baby girl. The Dyaks, the non-Malay tribes people of Borneo, are also active in the baby market. A case that came to my attention involved a Dyak woman who had a new baby but insufficient money for her lying-in period. She sold her five-year-old daughter for 500 local dollars, or the equivalent of $133 U.S.

The Malays and the Dyaks have the reputation for treating their slave children better than the Chinese do. They honor girls more, and inheritance often passes through the girls.

Sometimes a child is adopted because a family really wants it, but even in such cases it is paid for. Usually the purpose is to obtain a slave, an extra worker in the family. If the slave is a girl, and attractive, a marriage may eventually be arranged with one of the sons. It is also possible that the girl will be used as a prostitute, to bring in a few extra dollars.

In nearly every case the slave child is mistreated, frequently it is beaten. Sarawak law provides that all "adoptions" must be registered, but little effort is made to enforce this. Rather it would seem that some government officials ignore violations just as they do the opium trade, because of local custom and tradition.

There are only two children's homes in Sarawak and both are affiliated with the Christian Children's Fund. The one in Kuching is operated by the Salvation Army, that in Sibu by the Methodist Mission. At these homes and in talks with missionaries I heard many typical stories of slavery.

One day a prominent citizen appeared at the back door of a missionary's home. With him was an eleven-year-old girl who had run away from her mistress the evening before. With a few belongings tied in a sarong she had walked the three miles to town rather than ride the bus where she might have been recognized and returned to the leading citizen for whom she "worked."

"She says she will jump in the river rather than go back again," the prominent citizen told the missionary. "It's hard for me to help her because that man for whom she works is from the same city in China as I am and he would be offended."

It transpired that the girl had been sold by her brother in order to work off a family debt. The full tragedy of modern child slavery can best be understood from the uncorrected translation of the girl's story, provided me by the children's home where she now lives.

> When I was very small, I don't know my age, my mother died and soon then my father too. I was given to a family of my father's friends as a slave girl. . . . At first I was happy there, but after a while my mistress became very cruel to me. When I did wrong she often scolded me and beat me. When a duck or chicken was lost or died she struck me with all sorts of sticks. Once when I was so badly struck that I could not move, I found my body was all wounded. I felt pain in all parts of me. So I thought that I could not bear the ill treatment of my mistress any more. . . . I ran through the jungle until I came to a small cottage, where the people helped me escape to the town. I then went to the government hospital for investigating my wounded body. There I met an American missionary who pitied me when I showed her all my wounds. She received me into the Children's Home and helped me to study in the Methodist School.

The manner in which this girl's fate was settled indicates the part that slavery still plays in Chinese life. The girl's owner came to the missionary with various other eminent citizens to ask that the girl be returned, that legal action initiated by the missionary be dropped because of the family's standing in the community. They could not afford to lose face! Let the girl come back, she would henceforth be treated kindly.

The missionary replied that since they were prominent citizens there was all the more reason to carry the case to court. Then the delicate health of the cruel mistress was emphasized. A prison sentence would be very bad for her. The case was dropped, but the British Colonial Government made out papers legally giving the girl to the Methodist Mission for protection.

Thus a typical slave girl of Borneo was saved. There are hundreds like her among the 220,000 Chinese of Sarawak. In many cases, perhaps in most, the children can be helped if someone comes forward as their advocate. Colonial authorities are co-operative if there is evidence of mistreatment, and often the evidence is there for all to see in the welts and bruises that cover half-starved bodies.

There is an official known as the Protector of Women and Girls who will take legal action if charges are preferred. Unfortunately, as in the case just cited, it is seldom that anyone will give needed evidence. Major Elsie Willis, in charge of the Salvation Army Home at Kuching, told me that it is not unusual for people to come to the Home and ask for a small girl to be their "daughter." When it is suggested to them that if they want a child it might be better to have their own baby, they invariably reply, "But a baby needs too much attention." Major Willis told me that she does not agree to any adoptions. Invariably, in the past, follow-up investigations have revealed mistreatment and actual slavery, and all adopted children have come back into the Home under an order giving them government protection.

Ownership of slave children sometimes becomes complicated, and even leads into legal involvement. Major Willis told me a typical story. Ah Kiaw was sold merely because she was a girl and her parents did not want her. Later her owner sold her to another woman for $600, local currency. Within a week the new owner decided that Ah Kiaw was a poor investment and tried to get her money back. The legal battle ended in the office of the Protector of Women and Girls. Ah Kiaw was sent to the Salvation Army Home on a protection order, the two women were told to settle their financial problem elsewhere.

But the problem still remains of where such children can go if they are liberated. The two CCF-affiliated Homes in Sarawak presently can care for seventy-five children. Of these only twenty-one were being sponsored by Americans in 1956. As in Malaya the responsibility of caring for these children is an expensive one; for there are no public schools which they may attend. The thirty children in the Methodist Children's Home at Sibu must attend Methodist Mission schools if they are to receive an education.

Along with the need for liberating and caring for slave children, there is also a tremendous need of foundling homes in Sarawak, as in other areas heavily populated by Chinese. In hard times (and now that the price of pepper and rubber is down, times are especially difficult) there is an annual crop of illegitimate children and other unwanted and surplus babies. The Children's Homes of Sarawak are not prepared to take in newborn babies; new buildings and trained staff members would be necessary.

And the fate of unwanted babies, or those who for economic reasons cannot be kept, is obvious: the baby

Chinese children with educational facilities. No effort has been made to stop the malicious practice of selling children into a life of slavery.

In Sarawak, British North Borneo, there is an excellent home for juvenile delinquents. But only those teenagers who get into trouble, who eventually appear in juvenile court, can get into the home. For the orphaned or needy young Chinese who does not get into trouble there is no place to go. Also in North Borneo it is possible to buy opium in every town. The attitude seems to be that opium has always been there, is a part of local tradition; therefore, the trade should not be curtailed.

Except for one home for blind children operated by the Church of England, all the homes of Singapore and Malaya are run by the Salvation Army. And except for one babies' home in Singapore, the homes are in ancient buildings where children are badly crowded, sleeping sometimes thirty and forty to a room. The exception is of interest, for it was made possible by the gift of a rich Chinese, brother of one of Singapore's most ardent pro-communist Chinese businessmen.

Most of the boys and girls in the homes of Malaya come from unbelievably sordid backgrounds. Typical is the story of seven-year-old Moi Suwei. After her mother died, her father married again. The stepmother murdered the father and the little girl was left with a grandmother who was a leading communist terrorist in the jungles near Ipoh.

Or there is the story of two children, a girl aged four, a boy of six. The children's mother died and the father refused to work. Until juvenile authorities placed the children in a home, they supported their father by begging among the brothels of Singapore.

special worship facilities, a diet in accordance with Moslem faith. Obviously this makes operation of non-Moslem homes for Malay children difficult if not impossible.

In addition, the easygoing Malay is not likely to get into trouble. It is the Chinese teenager rather than the Malay who is found in Singapore's juvenile court. It is the young Chinese who frequently becomes involved in opium smuggling, in terrorist activities.

There are unbelievably wealthy Chinese in Southeast Asia, men like George Lee of Singapore, owner of the largest Chinese-language newspaper outside China, proprietor of rubber plantations, agent for Nash cars, Frigidaire, Admiral products. At the same time there are thousands of Chinese like Wang Tak An of Borneo, a young widow dying of TB, desperately trying to find someone to adopt her baby. For she knows that in the manner of local Chinese, her relatives will sell the child into slavery after her death.

In the nations of Southeast Asia there are thirteen orphanages affiliated with the Christian Children's Fund. A total of 531 children are sponsored by Americans. In Vietnam there is a home for refugee children of the Indo-China war. In Indonesia there is a home for children of mixed Dutch-Indonesian or Chinese-Indonesian blood. In all the other eleven orphanages, except for an occasional Tamil or a child from an aboriginal mountain tribe, the children are Chinese.

The problems of children are especially acute in those parts of Southeast Asia under British control, partly because of the strange inconsistencies of British rule. Thus, in Singapore there is one of the most complete cradle-to-grave welfare programs in the world, with tremendous new low-cost housing developments and free hospitalization. Yet for a century no effort was made to provide the happiest girls at Anyang, physically as robust as any other child in the home.

There are an even score of children at Anyang who came unknown and nameless. Wherever there has been war, in Japan, in China, in Korea, this is a frequent occurrence. Sometimes the child is given a name descriptive of his or her arrival. Thus a little boy, found abandoned under a chestnut tree at Anyang, is to this day known as "Little Chestnut." But more frequently the people of war-torn Asia show their deep longing for peace and tranquillity in the names they give their nameless waifs. An Hua-sil means "Little Flower of Peace."

6

The Overseas Chinese

THE war in Korea ended in 1953. The war in Indo-China ended in 1954. The war in the jungles of Malaya almost ended in 1955, but keeps sputtering on in occasional paroxysms of ambush and murder. For the ten million overseas Chinese in Southeast Asia, these wars are vitally significant. Even the Chinese in Singapore have a stake in happenings in Korea, four thousand miles away. The Chinese are caught in the middle of these shooting wars, in their sometimes strange economic effects. Thus the Korean war thrust the price of pepper sky high; the Chinese pepper growers were prosperous; the price of babies on the baby market hit a low.

Except in Indo-China with its 600,000 refugees, the known problems of children in Southeast Asia are largely confined to the Chinese. In part this is because centuries ago the apostles of Mohammed did a thorough missionary job in Malaya, Borneo, Indonesia. In areas under British control the right of the Malay to his faith, undisturbed, is a part of ancient treaties, made between the British and local sultans. It is almost impossible for Christian agencies to assist Moslem children who might need assistance. And very few Malays seek help. If a Malay child is taken into an orphanage the law provides that he must be provided

Mixed-blood children of Elizabeth Saunders Home in Japan, at the entrance to the Tunnel of Tragedy.

Three-year-old Helokazu, momentarily unhappy GI baby.

A Negro-Japanese child and two white-Japanese children.

A roof-top slum in Hongkong, city of two million refugees.

Three-year-old Andrea (in stroller), illegitimate child of an Indian student and an Austrian girl. Children's Village, Austria.

John C. Caldwell travels by reindeer sled en route to the Riutila
Home in Arctic Lapland.

Chinese orphans, Fanling Babies Home, Hongkong.

Mr. Mills, the Bulldozer-preacher.

A Chinese orphan of Singapore, rescued from Communist terror-
ists in the Malayan jungle.

Korea has its GI babies, too.

This girl was sold into slavery after her parents were killed by head hunters in Borneo.

Anglo-Indian children on the way to church at the Dr. Graham
Homes on the Indo-Tibetan border.

Ten-year-old Pasqualina Esposito of Naples' Casa Materna receives a package from her American sponsor.

Russian orphan children at the Foyer des Enfants, Paris.

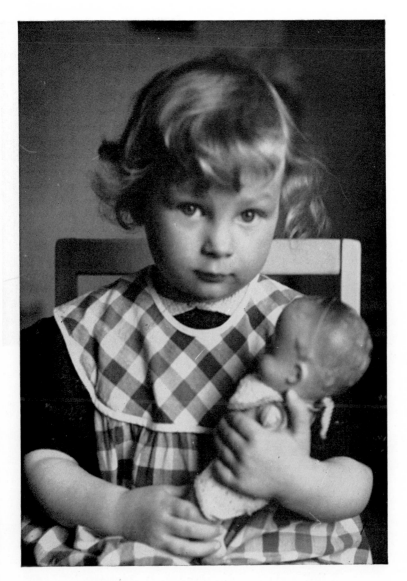

Three-year-old Helena of Lapland, an abandoned child.

Susie Skinner—a first hello to America.

market. Perhaps the baby will be fortunate, will be bought by a family who wants a child. Perhaps a Dyak or Malay family will be the purchaser. But more likely the child will become a slave, to be beaten and starved, or a juvenile prostitute.

Half-castes, Outcastes

IN INDIA, more than in any other nation in Asia, one sees evidence of starvation and mass poverty. There are the bloated bellies that denote real starvation, the ragged beggars who totter about more dead than alive. On any night, in any one of India's great cities thousands of people sleep on the streets. The more prosperous have mats, or even an occasional cot to place upon the sidewalk. But others sleep on the cobblestones without covering. On the forty-five-minute ride from Calcutta's Dum Dum Airport into the city, thousands of homeless can be seen sleeping on the streets. In spring and summer it is no privation to sleep out of doors. But in January and February there is a biting, penetrating cold, bringing discomfort and suffering to the thousands who are homeless.

Among these are thousands of children. The Christian Children's Fund is helping nearly nine hundred homeless in nine orphanages. But with the coming of independence there is less and less that can be done by Western agencies for the children of modern India. With independence there has been a rise in the spirit of communalism. The orphaned or half-orphaned child belonging to one of India's many sects and racial groups may desperately need institutional care, and the care may be available. But with increasing frequency relatives and friends belonging to the same sect will not allow the child to receive that care. Every sect, every group, tries to build up its numbers to be able to become better able to compete against the many other groups. The child who enters an orphanage, whether it be government or privately supported, is lost to the group. Frequently a mother may be unable to support a fatherless child and may wish to place the child in a home, but is unable to do so because communal interests transcend the interest of the child.

The riots that swept India in 1956 were a broad reflection of growing communalism. People were objecting to changes in the boundaries of states that would lessen the influence of language groups.

But there are two groups in India in which communalism plays little part, among which the need is desperate and much can be and is being done. These are the half-castes and the outcastes of the land. These groups have no organization to keep their members within the community, no overriding jealousies to keep needy children from receiving help. In fact there are few who even care whether help is received.

The half-castes of India, loosely called Anglo-Indian, number 111,000. They have a mixed ancestry, the West on one side and the East on the other—whether Indian, Nepalese, Sikkimese, Bhutanese or Tibetan.

The Anglo-Indian has provided the theme for numerous novels in recent years; and, true to life, most of the novels end in tragedy. For every successful union between East and West there have been a dozen unsuccessful. But since India gained its independence, the problem of the "Anglos" has become more acute with each passing year.

Under British rule many Anglos had positions of importance. Many categories in the Indian Civil Service were reserved for them. Any educated Anglo could be assured of a job in the postal service or on the railways. Since independence, the formerly reserved posts have been taken by persons who do not have the handicap of British ancestry. Slowly the Anglo-Indian has been pushed from the top to the bottom of the economic heap. Able a decade ago to live in the best sections of India's great cities, the Anglo has now been pushed into virtual ghettos.

I have visited the Anglo-Indian slums of Calcutta where thousands live in conditions of frightful squalor. I saw a family of four living on a veranda, open to the monsoon rains and with a total living space of twelve feet by six feet. I have seen mother and children camped in Calcutta's railroad station, their only home for months, perhaps even years. I have visited the homes of more prosperous Anglos, those who have perhaps two rooms for a family of six, eight or ten. More often two families will live in two or three rooms.

Miss Lucy Lucas, a social worker for the Scotch Presbyterian Mission, who was my guide through the Calcutta slums, told me that in lesser degree the conditions are duplicated in Bombay, Madras, New Delhi.

Whether in Calcutta, Tokyo, or Naples, slums breed TB, crime, prostitution—and orphans. The Anglo-Indian slums of India are no exception, and the plight of the children they spawn is tragic. But a magnificent effort is being made to help the young Anglos, and is receiving support from many Americans through the Christian Children's Fund.

It began many years ago with the Reverend J. A. Graham, a Scottish Presbyterian missionary among the mountain people in the Himalayan foothills. Touched by the plight of the needy and destitute Anglo-Indian children of encounters between British tea planters in Assam and the women who toiled in the fields, Dr. Graham took in two whom he found wandering in a bazaar and thus laid the foundations for the Dr. Graham's Homes of Kalimpong, West Bengal.

Kalimpong is in a corner of India that thrusts itself into the Himalayas. On the west is the Kingdom of Nepal. The border of Sikkim lies a few miles away. To the north is Tibet, and to the east and north the exotic little Kingdom of Bhutan, a country without roads, without a wheeled vehicle of any kind.

Kalimpong is on an outer spur of the Himalayas, 350 miles north of Calcutta. The visitor flies to Bagdogra, then goes on by car, forty miles up one of the most exciting roads in the world. It climbs from near sea level to 4,500 feet, passing up the valley of the roaring Teesta River, through magnificent jungles and scattered bazaars to Kalimpong. This resort city has as its background the mighty 15-mile barrier of snowy peaks that screens India from Tibet, thirty miles north. Immediately opposite the city is Kanchenjunga, third highest mountain in the world, towering straight up from the valley of the Teesta River to an elevation of 28,166 feet. All about are other massive peaks: Kabru, 24,002 feet; Trisul, 23,360 feet.

Because of its proximity to Tibet, Kalimpong has become a great trading center into which the Tibetan caravans come with their loads of wool. It is exotic, its bazaar teeming with people of many tribes. There are husky Tibetans, huge gold and jade rings in their ears; the mountain tribes people known as the Letchas; Nepalese, who wear rings in their noses; the people from neighboring Sikkim and Bhutan. There are Bengali traders from the lowlands of India, and now also there is a Communist Chinese trade mission, swarming with mysterious men who go back and forth across the Tibetan border on mysterious missions.

The Dr. Graham's Homes lie along the sides and the crest of Deola Hill, high above the main bazaar. The work that Dr. Graham began in 1900 with two Anglo-Indian waifs has expanded into one of the largest orphanages in the world. The property covers over 500 acres, the home cares for 550 children. There are nine boys' cottages, seven girls', a school, church, hostel for older boys, Lucia King cottage for babies and toddlers, a hospital— all combining to make a veritable children's town in the Himalayas.

Since its establishment it has cared for 3,600 Anglo-Indian children. Since independence, the need is greater than ever and there is not enough financial help.

I visited the Children's City in the Snows because it is among the largest affiliated with the Christian Children's Fund, receiving in 1956 over $15,000 from Americans who have sponsored Anglo-Indian children.

The children live thirty to a cottage, with one house mother for each fifteen children. Twenty per cent were fathered by the tea planters who live in nearby Assam. The mothers? Generally simple peasant women, workers in the fields. The attitude of most of the fathers is typified by one who recently brought a child, saying, "Here is fifty dollars. Take the brat. I never want to hear of her again."

There are three children of one family, their father dying of TB, who were found by social workers living on a railroad platform. There are five children of the H. family who were abandoned by their father. There is the son of a British telegraph operator in Lhasa, capital of Tibet. And even in faraway Kalimpong the American soldier of World War II has done his bit; there is one child fathered by an American soldier who visited the area on leave.

The Dr. Graham's Homes form a city within itself, with over one thousand mountain tribes people living on the property, helping with the crops. It is directed by Dr. James Duncan, a second-generation missionary to India, and its staff includes sixty men and women of a half dozen nationalities: British, Canadians, Australians, New Zealanders, Americans, and, of course, Indians.

In addition to the five hundred acres on Deola Hill, the Homes own another twenty-five acres in the valley of the Riili River where it is possible to grow pineapples, bananas and other fruits. As much as possible the Homes produce all the food for the children, including most of the milk. But the government does not provide as much help as it once did, and Dr. Jimmy Duncan and his staff face a constant battle to make ends meet. If it were possible to operate all the cottages, a total of 640 children could be taken in. But two cottages have remained closed for several years because of lack of funds.

The job of the Dr. Graham's Homes does not end when a boy or girl completes an education at Kalimpong. The nationalism of modern India makes it more and more difficult for the boys and girls to find a place in India. The Homes maintain a hostel in Calcutta where the boys may live. Lucy Lucas, welfare worker attached to the Homes but stationed in Calcutta, helps the girls find positions. But one measure of the problem is the fact that more and more second-generation children are finding their way into the Homes.

With Lucy Lucas I visited the homes of several graduates who have had to send their children to Kalimpong.
In some cases it is the illness or death of a parent that
makes this necessary. In most cases it is because of the
Anglo's limited chance to make a decent living. Unable
to get a job that pays a living wage, the graduate of the
Dr. Graham's Homes too frequently ends up in the slums
of Calcutta, there to breed more children who eventually
become orphans, half-orphans, or destitute candidates for
Kalimpong.

Jimmy and Molly Duncan are doing all that they can
to place their graduates. Some of the boys go to England
and join the British armed services. A growing number
are going to New Zealand and Australia. But Australia
makes it difficult by insisting that any Anglo who comes
must be 50 per cent "white." This means that only the
product of first-generation unions between Indian women
and Englishmen have an opportunity. And a large proportion of present-day Anglos are three-fourths Indian and
one-fourth British.

The Anglos have in part created their own problems.
When Britain ruled India and they were on the top of the
economic heap, many refused to learn Indian dialects.
They looked down upon their Indian countrymen. Even
today the Anglo children have to be persuaded of the
necessity of doing their own housework. They have to
be made to see that if they are to have a chance of happiness in India, they must forget their white blood and become real Indians. To accent this, Dr. Graham decreed
that all the children should go barefoot like 99 per cent of
their countrymen. His own children also went without
shoes. One of the strange sights at the homes today is
to see the children dressed for church—but barefoot.

But it is doubtful if most of the Anglos will ever find a secure place in India. As in the case of the mixed-blood children of Japan, places must be found elsewhere for these intelligent children. Great Britain and the Commonwealth nations can take a few each year. But perhaps the real solution for the Anglo lies in Latin America. There, where there is little race prejudice, it might be possible for hundreds to find jobs and a decent life far from the prejudices of today's India. Yet such a program requires money, much money. And there has been so little knowledge of the problem facing the Anglo-Indians that support would be difficult to obtain. Remember that to date it has not even been possible to reopen all of the cottages on Deola Hill.

It would not be fair to say that the Government of India has completely abandoned its 111,000 Anglo-Indians. For a period immediately after independence it provided no support whatsoever. Now each year the Central Government gives ten thousand rupees, or $2,000, and the Government of West Bengal sixty thousand rupees in support of the Dr. Graham's Homes. In contrast to these amounts, sponsors in faraway America are giving over $15,000, or the equivalent of 75,000 rupees annually. The rest of the thousands of dollars needed each year comes from friends in Great Britain and the Commonwealth, from a few people in India who are able to help.

One hundred and eleven thousand people is but a tiny drop in the massive stream of India's population. The children they produce and those being added each year by the tea planters of Assam are numerically unimportant in comparison to the other millions in India who need help.

But the Anglo-Indians are rapidly becoming a forgotten

by-product of colonialism. There are others like them, in Indo-China, Malaya, Indonesia. Collectively we call them Eurasians, and, as I have noted previously, among the colonial powers responsible for producing them, only the French in Indo-China have a sense of responsibility toward them.

Given help, the Anglo-Indian can make a contribution to any country. Those who have been fortunate enough to get good training have done well as doctors, nurses, professional people in every walk of life. Jimmy Duncan's files are filled with success stories.

But there is not enough money to help all those who need help. Each February a new "class" enters the Dr. Graham's Homes. In 1956 there were sixty new children, most of them gathered from Calcutta's slums. But for each of these sixty, three were turned away.

For the most part, if these half-castes are to have a chance, they must receive help from the people of the Western world. They have become unfortunate symbols of colonialism, unwanted in the land of their birth.

The Anglos at least do not die unmourned; their lot is easier than that of their brothers-in-misery, the outcastes of India. For every half-caste there are a hundred, even a thousand, outcastes.

India has made strides in removing the stigma of caste but there is still far to go. There are people who are outcastes merely because in the dim past, for reasons not now discernible, lowly tasks were reserved for their ancestors, and generation after generation this differentiation has been maintained. There are others who might just as well be termed outcastes simply because of their poverty, because of the depressed conditions under which they have lived for generations. From a practical standpoint there are millions of outcastes in India; for there are millions who are utterly depressed, who must struggle from day to day, generation after generation, to find enough to eat.

The Indian Government (which unofficially plays up America's own "caste" problems) has made numerous legal moves to free the depressed people from their bondage. There are compulsory education areas and fee concessions for higher education. People once bound to the land or to allotted tasks are technically freed from serfdom; they have been granted temple-entry privileges, a matter of considerable importance to non-Christians.

But with all these improvements, ingrained customs and prejudices are not easily forgotten. This is true of our own South, though we have but a few decades of custom and prejudice to combat, while in India oppression and caste are generations old.

Nowhere in India is there a more thrilling experiment in combating the prejudice of centuries than at the Alwaye Settlement, in Cochin-Travancore State, on the Malabar Coast of extreme Southwest India, an area that desperately needs help.

The Alwaye Settlement is wholly owned and operated by the Christian Children's Fund. It was founded in 1927 by an English missionary but came upon difficult times. CCF took over management in 1951. Covering seventy acres of rich land, the Settlement raises rice, mangos, bananas and tapioca. It cares for 190 orphans, operates a high school with an enrollment of 290, while the local village elementary school is in a CCF-owned building. A measure of India's educational needs is that there are 450 children in the elementary school and but two teachers.

The Alwaye Settlement is interesting and significant for a number of reasons. It is located in an area where there is an indigenous Christian Church, supposedly founded by St. Thomas in the second century. The State of Cochin-Travancore lies along the Malabar Coast of the Indian Ocean and is partly made up of rich and fertile tropical land, partly of the rugged inland mountain range called the Western Ghats. The Ghats are sparsely populated, but the area along the coast and inland to the Ghats is among the most densely populated in the world. Along with this dense population goes an immense number of unemployed. The only kind of high school education available in Travancore is a literary one. In an average year only one of ten high school graduates can find a job. Thus year after year, the number of "literary" unemployed grows larger.

There is a direct relationship between this fact and the fact that Cochin-Travancore is one of the centers of communist activity and strength in India. Thousands of unemployed young people listen to the communist story, hopeful that it may somehow answer their problems, that through communism it may be possible to find employment and security.

It is for this reason that the Alwaye Settlement is important; for it does not seek merely to add to the "educated unemployed." At Alwaye an effort is being made not only to salvage the orphaned and abandoned children of the depressed classes, but to train boys and girls of all classes so that they can go out into society to become much-needed mechanics, electricians, carpenters, seamstresses, secretaries. Cochin-Travancore desperately needs young people who are able and willing to work with their hands.

The Alwaye Settlement was of especial interest to me because of the young American couple who direct it. Bill and Thelma Henry are typical of the missionary of practical type so needed in the world today. Bill was an air force pilot during the war, flying the dangerous Hump route between India and China. When peace came, Bill returned to his native Iowa to complete his schooling under the GI Bill. He could have had an excellent position with a commercial airline; indeed, he flew for a time with one. But for Bill and Thelma, who was an experienced schoolteacher, life had to have some meaning other than a big salary.

During the war Bill Henry had come to realize the tremendous needs of this sprawling country of India. Purely by chance he heard about the Christian Children's Fund, applied for a job and ended up as Superintendent of the Alwaye Settlement. Thelma, with her schoolteaching experience, is a valuable member of the team.

The Henrys have made Alwaye into one of the unique institutions of India. It is far more than a home for orphans. Mr. P. J. Thomas, former chief economic adviser to Prime Minister Nehru of India, stated after a visit that "The Alwaye Settlement and the Vellore Medical Mission are doing more good in India than all the money given by the U.S. Government to the Indian Government."

It is not difficult to understand why Dr. Thomas might make such a statement. On the twenty acres of Alwaye's land devoted to rice, Bill Henry has managed to average an annual crop twice that raised on the paddies of neighboring farmers. Bill is not an agricultural expert. He has merely applied a little book learning to rice culture, and now each year more Indian farmers are coming to visit Alwaye's paddies, to see what miracles are being performed there by a young ex-air force pilot and his Indian helpers. Now it is Bill's hope to obtain some folidol, the miracle insecticide developed in West Germany and found to be sure death for the rice-stem borer. With folidol it will be possible to triple the yield.

But perhaps the most significant contribution Alwaye is making is in human relations, in showing the young of Travancore that it is not beneath one's dignity to work with the hands, to show also that the children of the depressed classes can work side by side with those of other classes with mutual benefit rather than contamination. At Alwaye boys and girls who are descended from the primitive Dravidian tribes are able to work with the sons and daughters of Syrian Christian families.

The vocational phases of Alwaye's program need a great deal more development if the Settlement is to make the contribution it can to the community and the country. At present twelve boys are studying tailoring, ten simple electrical engineering, a half dozen the operation and use of a tractor. Others are studying banana and tapioca culture. Every boy must spend one hour each day in manual labor—either in his chosen work, or in repairing roads or the playground. It is strange to Americans, who delight in the manual labor afforded by working in one's garden, or in doing a little painting around the house, that there are people who would literally rather starve than use their hands. This is a curse not only of India but of other places in the Far East. At Alwaye boys are learning the dignity of manual labor, and in an area where there are thousands of educated unemployed, this is important.

What kind of children find their way to this palm-dotted

spot on the Indian Ocean? While visiting Alwaye I obtained the life stories of many of the 186 boys and girls then living at the Home.

Thirteen-year-old K. Valsalan has been at Alwaye three years. His parents were laborers (outcastes) in the rubber estates at Peermade, seven thousand feet up in the Western Ghats. The father died of malaria while the boy was very young. The mother brought the boy to a government home for destitute people and within a year died of malaria. Children cannot be cared for in such homes, and the little boy found his way to Alwaye and a CCF sponsor.

K. V. George lost his father, a mountain hunter, when he was three. The mother worked as a domestic servant, doing the menial tasks befitting an outcaste. She became ill and decided to seek help from a relative who lived far away. With K. V. and an older daughter she began the long walk. After a while she became exhausted and sat down beneath a tree, and within a few hours died of starvation and exhaustion. A passer-by found the children and took them in until permanent homes could be found. K. V. has now been at Alwaye almost four years.

Kunjammini Thomas, age eight, was brought to another orphanage when she was two years old by a man claiming to be her grandfather. The man never returned to inquire about the child. She was brought to Alwaye when St. Thomas, the original orphanage, could no longer care for her.

Lydia Abraham, age thirteen, is a child without a background except that she is from the depressed classes. At the age of eight she was a domestic servant and was brought to Alwaye badly beaten. In her first year at the settlement little Lydia was frightened of everyone—the matrons, the other girls. But as the memories of beatings and the tragic past receded she became one of the happiest girls in the Home.

These are typical case histories of Alwaye children, perhaps two thirds of them coming from the truly out-caste groups, one third coming from the Syrian Christian families which make up a considerable part of Cochin-Travancore's population.

What happens to similar children, faced with the loss of one or both parents, if they have not the refuge that Alwaye provides? They are simply at the mercy of an un-kind society, or a society blocked off from them by cen-turies-old custom. As caste operates, people are unable to change their lot themselves. Government, as I have said, is moving slowly toward the day when these social barriers will be removed. But today, unless there is a place like Alwaye championing the children who are in every way down and out, they can scarcely rise above the position of the family into which they were born.

From that standpoint alone, the Alwaye Settlement is of tremendous significance in India's slow struggle to-ward equality and justice for all.

As fine as is the work being done at Alwaye, much more could be accomplished if sufficient funds were avail-able. There are 190 children at the Settlement, most of them with CCF sponsors. Thus individual Americans are giving a total of $1,900 monthly. In addition, the Christian Children's Fund provides money from its general fund for building, for the payment of staff salaries.

Even with this help there are many things of value that cannot be done. A first-class auto-diesel school, capable of turning out the mechanics that India needs, would be a significant contribution to the whole country. There should be a full secretarial course for girls, all of whom could then find employment in business.

Alwaye faces the same problem as the Dr. Graham's Homes in placing its graduates. In former years many young people from the Malabar Coast went to Ceylon or to Southeast Asia to seek their fortunes. But nationalism, in India and in the other nations, makes this increasingly difficult. The young are more and more bound to their native state where only good training can overcome the hindrance of birth that shackles so many. Unless the high school graduate is exceptionally well trained in a field of work needed in India, he has two strikes against him.

It does little good to graduate more young people from high school, for they merely join the army of unemployed and become easy targets for communist propaganda. There are job opportunities, but for young men and women trained to work with their hands as well as their brains.

In spite of the fact that Cochin-Travancore is one of India's major communist centers, Bill and Thelma Henry have made Alwaye liked and appreciated. They have entered a difficult situation with unusual tact. Given more support, they could make of Alwaye a much larger institution. There are many more children of Syrian Christian families who need the help that Alwaye can give. There are innumerable orphans and half-orphans from the depressed classes who could be helped—if there were more cottages and money for an increased staff.

It is a measure of our own failing that it is difficult to find enough sponsors for the so-called colored peoples of the world. A study of the appeal advertising through which Christian Children's Fund finds its sponsors reveals many interesting facets of the American mind. For instance, those who are religiously and politically conservative give more than those who are liberal. The family living in a small town is more likely to sponsor a child than one living in a city. Men and women of moderate income give more generously than the rich. And most givers, regardless of religion, politics, and residence, prefer to sponsor a white child or a Korean or Chinese.

The Alwaye Settlement needs more sponsors, so that more children may be taken in. But it also needs the large gifts of money which will enable it to fulfill its tremendous potential. Here, it seems to me, would be a logical place for one of our great foundations to make a grant. For the Alwaye Settlement is more than a Christian missionary enterprise. It is an experiment in human relations, in an area of tremendous need, among people who are largely Christian but who because of oppression and depression are terribly vulnerable to the appeal of communism.

8

Generations of the Faithful

FROM Beirut the road to Damascus climbs dizzily up the steep slopes of the Lebanon Mountains. From the pass high above the city the great hump of Mount Herman can be seen rising from the barren ridges of the Anti-Lebanon range. Between the two mountain ranges there is a broad and fertile valley. The Bikaa, it is called, and down the valley's center runs the Litani River.

The Damascus road winds down the eastern slopes of the Lebanon, crosses the twenty-odd miles of the Bikaa, climbs the Anti-Lebanon before plunging down again into the oasis of Damascus. At the foot of the Lebanon there is a road leading to the right, southward up the Bikaa and to the borders of Israel. Thirteen miles up the valley from the Damascus road, near the Arab village of Khirbet Kanafar, is the J. L. Schneller Home and School.

The story of the Schneller Home (officially known as the Syrian Orphanage, Lebanese Branch) is a chronicle of the faith and vision of a man who lived and worked a century ago, who passed that faith down through four generations of the Schneller family. In the story of the Schnellers one learns also of the tragedy of the Middle East, brought into sharp focus in 1956 but beginning decades ago.

I visited the Schneller Home on a bright day in January. The Bikaa Valley was warm but Mount Herman and the higher ridges of the Lebanon and Anti-Lebanon were crested with deep snow. I drank strong Arabian coffee with Pastor Hermann Schneller, walked with him among the new buildings of the Home, met and talked with Arab boys whose lives have been blighted by the Arab-Israeli wars. Everything at the Schneller Home is new, for all the original property of this home founded nearly a century ago was a casualty of the war.

The Schneller story began long before our Civil War and cannot be understood merely by visiting today's orphanage in the Bikaa Valley.

In the 1850's there lived in Württemberg, in southern Germany, a teacher whose name was Johann Ludwig Schneller. He was a good teacher and also much interested in church work. On Sundays the people of the town came to him and read the Bible while Schneller explained the text. In time this interest in the Bible led the young teacher into a decision. In 1854 Johann and his wife Magdalena came to Jerusalem to become missionaries among the Arabs.

The Schnellers purchased a small plot of land four kilometers from the gates of the Old City. They built a small cottage with the hope of starting a mission for the Moslems in the villages near Jerusalem.

But there were religious fanatics among the Moslem Arabs, and robbers roamed the hills around Jerusalem. One day Johann was attacked as he traveled to Jerusalem by donkey and was seriously wounded. A few weeks later the Schneller cottage was besieged by hostile Arabs. Johann and Magdalena built barricades of furniture. But when the Arabs attacked the door with axes, Johann was forced to use his gun. After this experience the young couple moved into Jerusalem.

It was several years before the Schnellers were able to move back to their cottage and take up their missionary work again. It was now 1860 and Johann's missionary work had brought discouragement and, it seemed to him, little result. But nearby events were occurring which were to shape Johann's life and that of his descendants.

There were many Christian Arabs living in Southern Lebanon, in the Mount Herman district. Suddenly Christian villages were attacked by fanatic Druzes. Thirty thousand Christians were massacred and the survivors fled to Beirut and Sidon where they lived in refugee camps, much like those of today. The killing stopped because Great Britain and France sent warships to Beirut. But the surviving Christian Arabs lived in sorrow and distress amid the sand dunes of the Mediterranean shore.

Johann Schneller heard of these events and was determined to help. It was then that God showed him his life's task: to care for the orphans of the Middle East. He visited the refugee camps and found many orphaned children in desperate need. But the Arabs were suspicious of the young German. He was able to find only nine boys he could help. These boys he took home to the little cottage. They traveled by boat to Jaffa, then by donkeyback across the barren mountains to Jerusalem.

Johann and the nine orphans arrived in Jerusalem on Martin Luther's birthday, November 11th, in 1860. The little house in the Jerusalem suburbs now became known as the Syrian Orphanage because the district from which the children came belonged at that time to the Turkish Province of Damascus in Syria.

When the refugees in Lebanon heard that the nine

orphans were learning to read and write they sent more
children to Johann and Magdalena. At the end of the first
year there were thirty children in the Syrian Orphanage.
And for several years Schneller traveled back to
Lebanon each summer to find more needy children. In
time his work attracted the attention of church people
in Europe. Old friends in Württemberg collected money,
sent blankets. A governing board was established for the
Syrian Orphanage. Headquarters were at Stuttgart first,
later at Köln am Rhein, and there it is to this day. Another
committee was established in Switzerland, and friends in
the United States organized a group to assist the growing
institution.

Within a few months the little cottage could no longer
house the children. Many girls, sisters of boys already
admitted, wanted to come to Jerusalem so it was necessary
to build a girls' home. When Johann Schneller found
many blind children begging in the cities of Lebanon and
Palestine, he built a home for the blind.

And the practical-minded young German also saw the
need for vocational training, realized that his boys and
girls would have little opportunity to make good unless
they learned a trade. Soon he had built a carpentry shop,
a smithy, a pottery, a printing establishment. Finally a
teacher's training college was added. What began in a
cottage on the outskirts of Jerusalem became one of the
largest Christian institutions in the Middle East. When
Johann Schneller died in 1896 the Syrian Orphanage
sheltered 180 boys and girls, had already graduated 500
trained workers.

The Schneller graduates made good because they were
among the few young Arabs trained for any profession.
Some worked in trades, others in the different Protestant

missions and schools. Others continued their studies with help from relatives and became doctors, lawyers, teachers and successful businessmen.

When Johann died, much beloved by the people— they called him Father Schneller—his place was taken by Theodor, his eldest son. A second son, Ludwig, took over directorship of the Syrian Orphanage Board at Cologne. And thus the Schneller dynasty passed into its second generation.

In 1898 a new and sad event added to the growth of the Orphanage. In that year the Turks began once again to persecute the Armenians who lived in Turkey. Thousands were slaughtered, and the Syrian Orphanage was asked if it could take in one hundred and forty Armenian orphans. The board agreed. But it was 1901 before new buildings could be erected. When the Armenian children arrived in that year there were three hundred and twenty children in the home. The workshops were transferred to new and larger quarters, new teachers were employed, a branch home to specialize in agricultural training was built on a plot of land Father Schneller had purchased near Jaffa.

In 1908, at the urging of American friends, it was decided to open another branch in Nazareth. Thus, following carefully the lines laid out by Johann Schneller, the Syrian Orphanage expanded.

But in 1910, soon after the fiftieth anniversary of the institution, fire destroyed the main buildings and chapel at Jerusalem. And soon after there came another blow. In 1914 the First World War broke out. The building program at Nazareth was well under way, the buildings in Jerusalem destroyed by fire had just been rebuilt.

With war and its uncertainties came swarms of locusts

which covered all the Middle East. The vineyards and vegetable gardens were destroyed. Only the wheat could be saved, for it was already ripe and too hard for the locusts' mouths. A severe famine came in the wake of the locusts. For a while the children lived on lupines, cooked for hours to take away the bitter taste. Director Theodor Schneller finally managed to find additional wheat at a price he could afford to pay. Not only did he feed the children—each day a thousand poor people of Jerusalem came to obtain free flour rations.

On December 16th, 1916, the British Army entered Jerusalem. And six months later the Syrian Orphanage was confiscated by military authorities, its staff members sent to Egypt to spend the remaining months of the war in internment camps as German nationals.

It was 1921 before Theodor Schneller returned from exile, to begin a period of unparalleled expansion. The home at Nazareth was completed. All the workshops were equipped with new machinery, a brick factory and mechanical trade school were opened. By 1927 the several branches of the Orphanage were caring for four hundred children and each year between four and six hundred boys and girls were turned away.

There were now several thousand Schneller alumni in the Middle East, eager to help the institution. They published a paper which was circulated all through the area, even in Europe and America. Once each year the alumni assembled at the Jerusalem Home. Many brought their children to be baptized by Theodor Schneller, others came to be married by their old Director. And now it was possible to fulfill still another of Father Schneller's wishes: to create a colony and congregation of former students.

Many graduates bought plots of land near the Orphanage, built their homes there.

In 1927, at year's end, Theodor Schneller handed over the administration of the Orphanage to his son Pastor Hermann Schneller. Thus, eighty-seven years after its founding, the Syrian Orphanage came under the direction of a third-generation Schneller.

For twelve years progress continued under Hermann Schneller but all this came abruptly to an end in August, 1939. Again Europe was plunged into war and again the Schnellers and their institution suffered. Most of the German staff members left for home soon after the war began. Hermann and four others stayed on, were interned, then released. For a while it appeared that the work could go on, the British seemed interested in keeping the Orphanage alive. There were financial problems because income from Europe was cut off. But with the help of the Boards in Switzerland and America, through the income of the orphanage farms, with the generous assistance of the American YMCA in Jerusalem it was possible to carry on the work. But this was only for a while. . . .

Suddenly in May, 1940, the British Military gave Hermann Schneller forty-eight hours to evacuate the institutions. This difficult task was fulfilled but it was not possible to find places for all the orphans, the blind children. Eighty boys were sent to Nazareth and forty to Bethlehem, where suitable rooms could be rented.

Hermann Schneller and his German co-workers were again interned. Like his father, Hermann was sent into exile but not to nearby Egypt—in 1941 Hermann Schneller was deported to Australia. There he lived in an internment camp but not merely for the war's duration. For reasons unknown to him, Schneller was not repatriated until 1948. He had not seen his family for eight years and three months.

The problems of the Syrian Orphanage had just started. In 1948 the Arab-Israeli war began and again the children and staff members became refugees. The section of Jerusalem in which the main home was located became a part of Israel and all the buildings were taken over. When fighting approached Nazareth, the Arab commander ordered the evacuation of the Nazareth Branch. Two teachers, Mr. Nasser and Mr. Haddad, fled to Lebanon with thirty boys by truck. They had with them a large tent. By the end of 1948 the tent was all that remained of Father Schneller's dream. Its buildings seized by the Israeli Government, its equipment lost, its boys and girls scattered, the Syrian Orphanage had been dealt a deadly blow.

But with help from the Lutheran World Federation, Hermann Schneller returned to the Middle East, arriving in Beirut on August 10th, 1949. With unbounded faith he opened a new home in Bethlehem, a new trades school on the Mount of Olives in the Arab section of Jerusalem.

These facilities could not begin to meet the needs of an Arab refugee population of 800,000. And it became obvious that it would be foolish to build large facilities in Bethlehem or Jerusalem so close to the Arab-Israeli border.

And so it was agreed to re-establish the Syrian Orphanage in Lebanon, far from border tensions and the fighting that flared intermittently.

Hermann Schneller was given the responsibility of locating the new home. He went to Lebanon in 1951 and rented a house at Zahle, the district town of the Bikaa, in the beautiful valley of the Litani River. There he found a small colony of former graduates and there in November, 1952, the Syrian Orphanage, Lebanese Branch, came into being.

At first there was room for only twelve boys. But when two buildings were completed in 1952 eighteen more were taken into the home. Meanwhile the Lutheran World Federation was negotiating with the Israeli Government about compensation for the property that had been seized. Again, the Schneller's nationality was against them. An agreement was finally concluded but the Israelis were in no mood to be generous with Germans. Compensation was agreed upon at six per cent of the original value, payable in ten annual installments.

The compensation was insufficient to build again the institution that had flourished for so long. It would not be enough to rebuild the trades school that had proved so useful to the children of the Middle East, or to re-establish the teachers' training school. This was a heavy blow to Hermann Schneller, but like his grandfather he is a man of great faith.

By 1954 Hermann Schneller had erected a new building, in 1955 half of another building was completed. Money was raised for new carpentry shop equipment. When I visited the new Schneller Home in 1956 it was caring for eighty-nine boys.

A new staff has been recruited, including the wife and the sister of Hermann Schneller. And a fourth generation Schneller is now on the job. Hans Schneller, an agricultural engineer, great-grandson of Johann Ludwig Schneller, is in charge of developing a new farm and agricultural training program at Khirbet Kanafar.

The new home at Khirbet Kanafar in the Bikaa Valley

is but a shadow of the institution founded by Johann Schneller and enlarged by his son and grandson. In 1939 the Syrian Orphanage owned twenty-three hundred acres, with seventy buildings valued at $13,000,000. The staff consisted of sixty teachers. At Khirbet Kanafar there are 160 acres, six buildings valued at $150,000, a staff of eighteen.

But already the Schnellers are planning big things for the future. Alumni in Amman have asked the Board of Directors to open a school and home in Jordan's capital city. A Jordan Alumni Society has been formed and even though most of the members are refugees they have collected $1,500 for a building fund.

The Board of Directors, feeling that Father Schneller would want it so, have agreed to the request of the Jordan alumni and have purchased a small plot of land. The general idea is to build a trades school in Amman while concentrating on teacher training and vocational agriculture at Khirbet Kanafar. It will be a difficult job and the development will take years. A small beginning has been made under the supervision of still another member of the Schneller family, Lutheran Mission Inspector Ernst Schneller, brother of Hermann. But eventually it is planned that Hans, of the fourth generation, will be in charge of the Amman development.

The contribution of this remarkable family cannot be measured in terms of the small project at Amman, or the eighty-nine boys now at Khirbet Kanafar. Since Father Schneller began his work ninety-six years ago, six thousand boys and girls have received an education or vocational training. Schneller-trained men are found in every Arab nation. They man the pumping stations of the oil companies in the deserts; they are successful professional men in Jerusalem, Damascus, Beirut, Aleppo. In Amman there are two hundred Schneller graduates, including men prominent in Jordan's political and economic life. There are Schneller graduates in America, successful businessmen saved from death or a life as beggars.

Surely in no country has there ever been a family like the Schnellers. The impact of their lives through almost a century cannot be measured in terms of graduates, in dry statistics on the number of Arabs who have become Christians. With a faith that has carried them through war and internment, fire and massacres, they have made life better for thousands of Arabs, have made it possible for thousands to be physically and spiritually reborn.

Difficult and uncertain years lie ahead but Hermann Schneller has no fears. He told me, "Many difficulties will have to be overcome. But we trust that God will guide the work and, as He has allowed us to rebuild in the Lebanon, will also allow us to continue our Amman project so that this institution will be again, by His grace, a blessing for the poor and the orphans of the Near East."

Father Johann would be shocked at the numbers of "the poor and the orphans" in the Near East, at human misery of a magnitude he could not have imagined. At the latest count there are 904,000 Arab refugees. These ragged, hungry and disillusioned people live in desolate camps, kept alive by *seven cents a day* provided by the United Nations.

I saw their camps on the outskirts of Jerusalem and near Bethlehem. At Khirbet Kanafar I met nine-year-old Tallaa Hussein, a typical bit of the human flotsam that floats in the wake of the Arab-Israeli fighting.

Tallaa is the latest arrival at the Schneller Home. He was found wandering on the slopes of Mount Herman by Bedouin tribesmen. Tallaa lost both parents in the escape from Israel in 1949. He has been passed about by distant relatives, has spent most of his life in flight. When he arrived at the Schneller Home, Tallaa had never slept in a bed, had never been inside a house, had never worn a pair of shoes.

There are thousands like Tallaa. The Lutherans, through the Lutheran World Federation and more specifically through the German Lutheran Church, have done more for the children orphaned by the war than any other group. But they have barely touched the problem. There are now 1,000 applicants for places in the Schneller Home at Khirbet Kanafar. At Talitha Kumai, a Lutheran Home for girls on the outskirts of Bethlehem, I found this situation: 137 children but beds for only 101. On the home's waiting list there are 3,000 children.

The problem of the Arabs and their children will not be easily solved. Many of the children at Khirbet Kanafar and at the other Lutheran Homes receive help from American sponsors. But sponsorship is not enough—there must be money for new buildings at established homes and money for new homes. Americans have a responsibility in the Arab lands, for we have become deeply involved in the political developments that have produced the refugees. American generosity has enabled the Christian Children's Fund to help support nearly 10,000 Korean children, 2,300 Japanese and over 2,000 Chinese, to also build beautiful model homes in the Far East. But in the Middle East CCF is able to help less than 200 Arab children, has no building program.

And as in the Far East, the problem of the Arabs is a

continuing one. The refugees have no desire to stay in Jordan or Lebanon but it is unlikely that Israel will agree to their return. And so they will live on in the dreary camps until their destinies are decided in some new political explosion.

As tragic as is the plight of these people, there are equally tragic conditions among other displaced persons in the Middle East. Twenty miles down the Bikaa Valley from Khirbet Kanafar begin the settlements of another displaced nationality, people who have not seen their homeland for forty years. In their forty years of exile they have made some progress, have moved from tent cities into cities of shacks. But misery, hunger, disease, the uncertainty of the future are no less painful even if they be in a mansion. And there are no mansions at the Aindjar Settlement.

9

Miss Jacobsen's Secret Family

THE plane from Beirut to Jerusalem flies directly over the Schneller Home in the Bikaa Valley. Then the route lies over the lower slopes of Mount Herman, across the headwaters of the Jordan and into the Holy City. On the return flight the plane takes a more easterly course, across the Jordan near the head of the Dead Sea, on directly above Damascus and over the Bikaa Valley well to the northeast of the Schneller Home.

The road to Damascus lies below the plane now, and along the road are neat settlements. Aindjar is the name of one of these settlements. From the air it appears neat and trim, six hundred snowy white houses, laid out in a geometrical pattern. The Damascus road passes through the center of Aindjar just before the road leaves the valley to twist up the slopes of the Anti-Lebanon Mountains and down into the green oasis that is Syria's capital city.

But when Aindjar is visited, it is not as trim or as neat as it appeared from six thousand feet. The little houses are small indeed, each with one room and in some cases sleeping nine people in a space twenty feet by twelve feet. The roads are unpaved and muddy. Most houses have no running water, no indoor toilet facilities.

There are notable things about Aindjar. One is the remarkable proportion of children among its many inhabitants and the fact that the older children speak beautiful English. And among the many tiny cubicle-like homes there is a gleaming school, very new and perhaps the most modern in all the Middle East. Long residence in the Middle East is not required to realize that the adults on Aindjar's streets are not Arabs, that the children who frolic in the schoolyard are also not Arabs.

The Aindjar Settlement is one of many in Lebanon and Syria built by and for the 150,000 refugees from Turkish Armenia. Many of the refugees have been exiles for forty years. Among them are second- and third-generation displaced persons, people who never have and never will see their native land.

Aindjar's new school is a bright spot in this crowded rural slum. Built by the Christian Children's Fund in 1954, it is operated by Sisters of the Reformed Church of Switzerland. A few blocks from the school there is an orphanage, affiliated with CCF since 1950. One hundred and fifty children live in the Aindjar Orphanage, 126 of them sponsored by Americans.

Many of the Aindjar children are not orphans in the true sense. Generally a mother is alive, somewhere. The four thousand residents of the Settlement came in 1930, relocated in Aindjar by the French Government.

Aindjar is a paradise now in comparison to what the refugees had even a few years ago. Then there was no water, now there are communal faucets. Then there was no school, no medical facilities. The land, on the slopes of the Anti-Lebanon Mountains, was sterile desert. Now there are groves of apple trees from Switzerland, each family has a plot of land one hundred meters square. The rocky soil has been nursed and watered so that it does produce small garden plots.

CCF has made many of the changes possible. It has invested in Aindjar money equivalent to the sponsorship of 150 children for ten years. But CCF has been able to but scratch the surface of one of the most tragic refugee problems of the Middle East, the problem of the displaced Armenians, a people driven from their homes forty years ago and wandering from settlement to settlement ever since.

The children at Aindjar are fortunate. For they do have broad valleys and hills at their doorsteps. Elsewhere, in the cities of Lebanon and Syria, there are great Armenian slums, areas of unbelievable filth and poverty. The Armenian slums of Beirut lie on the city's northern outskirts. Here, in ramshackle buildings not fit for human habitation, ten and twelve people are crowded to a room. Inevitably the slums breed crime and tuberculosis, prostitution and illegitimacy.

The tragedy of Beirut's Armenian slums, the Aindjar Settlement, the plight of the Middle East's 150,000 refugees from a persecution most of us have forgotten, can be made to come alive through the remarkable story of a Danish woman, a nurse, who now is seventy-four years old and is completing a lifetime of service to the people of Armenia.

Maria Jacobsen arrived in Central Turkey in 1907, a missionary nurse assigned to a hospital operated by Americans. She was twenty-four years old. Her first station was in the city of Mezreh. Two years later the mission built a new hospital at the city of Harpoot and young Maria Jacobsen was placed in charge. Harpoot and Mezreh were located in Armenian sections of Turkey and the missionary hospitals served the Christian Armenians.

Throughout the nineteenth century there were periods when the Moslem Turks persecuted the Christian Armenians. The last great massacres came in 1898. Then for fifteen years there was a period of relative peace. But when World War I broke out in 1914 the peace between Turks and Armenians, never very stable, was threatened. Immediately after the outbreak of hostilities all Armenian men were taken as soldiers. Only men able to pay forty gold pounds were safe and this sum was demanded of the same men over and over. In 1915 all the Armenian men of Harpoot not already impressed into military service were rounded up at night, driven into the nearby hills and murdered. The slaughter was not confined to one city. All over Turkey, wherever there were Armenian communities, the men were killed. Only a small number succeeded in escaping.

In July, 1915, the persecution extended to the women and children. The Armenians in Harpoot were rounded up, told that they were to go to the city of Der Zor, a month's journey by foot over the mountains.

"We missionaries were unable to help," Maria Jacobsen told me. "The Turkish Government put soldiers at all our doors and even on the roofs of our houses. For six months we were unable to leave our homes. And most of the Armenians were killed, or died long before they reached Der Zor."

During the late summer of 1915 groups of Armenians from outlying villages were driven into Harpoot and in Miss Jacobsen's words, "gathered on a large place surrounded by a high wall. After six months we missionaries and the American Consul went to the place. But we found

only the sick and dying. On one side of the place there
was a long deep ditch into which they threw the dead. We
could do nothing. From these thousands of Armenians
the Turks took the women they liked and the children
and brought them to their homes as slaves."

This was a difficult period for a young woman, but at
least she was not alone. She had American colleagues. But
in 1917 the United States declared war on Germany and
her allies, including Turkey. The American missionaries
were given twenty-four hours to pack and were marched
out under military escort.

"When they left they asked me if I would stay behind,"
Miss Jacobsen told me. "They promised to come back as
soon as the war was over. And the war could not possibly
last more than six months. We had at that time forty
Armenian children, girls we had been able to hide in the
hospital. I could not think of leaving them. I agreed to
stay. The missionaries and the American Consul gave me
what money they had. And then they left. It was the seven-
teenth of May, 1917."

Maria Jacobsen did not see an American again for
twenty-five months. Indeed, for two years she hardly saw
a friendly face. During that lonely time she did things that
seemed impossible for one woman, even a whole mission
station, to accomplish. It is typical of Miss Jacobsen that I
would never have known of her exploits had it not been
that an Armenian teacher, who lived through the period,
told me.

First came a period of food shortage. Wheat, the basic
food of Central Turkey, became very scarce. What wheat
there was was hoarded by the merchants. Everyone had a
difficult time, including the Turks, who could no longer

feed the Armenian women and children taken as slaves two years earlier.

The women were killed and the children simply driven into the desolate mountains.

Late that summer starving children began to drift back into the city, searching for the missionaries. Three of the mission buildings were still in Miss Jacobsen's hands. But she did not dare openly to take the children in, fearing the Turks would then kill them. Miss Jacobsen was faced with the problem of how to save the children who lay ill and starving on the streets of the city.

But save them she did! Maria Jacobsen conceived a brilliant but dangerous solution. One whole section of the city, the section once inhabited by the Armenians, lay in ruins. The Turks never entered the area, for every home had long since been ransacked and picked over. Miss Jacobsen began to move children into the ruins by night.

After I had been told a bit of the story by the Armenian teacher in Beirut, I managed to get details from Miss Jacobsen.

"In each ruined house I put the children with one of the girls who had been hidden in the hospital in charge. Although from ten to fourteen children died each day, the number taken in was greater. Many were sick with scurvy. Some were so blown up you could not see what they looked like. I did not have anything to do this work with. The money left me was soon finished. But when the American missionaries reached Constantinople on their way home, they managed to send more money. There were two Armenians in a bank there. The Turks had kept them alive because they did not trust their own personnel."

For a while Miss Jacobsen had funds to buy wheat on

the black market. Meanwhile the children in her secret family increased, until in the late fall of 1917 she had over a thousand children hidden away in the ruins.

It was a tremendous responsibility for the young Danish woman. The children had to be coached never to talk; the very young ones must learn never to cry. Each section had its older boy or girl acting as monitor. Fires could be lit, but only at night and in the deep cellars.

"But the family of children grew and the price of wheat went higher. We could not find bread to keep alive. I then began to crush the wheat I could buy and boil it in water. But we had no greens—nothing but wheat and water. Our fuel was manure, gathered at night."

Now there were two thousand children in the ruins and more help was needed. Miss Jacobsen made the acquaintance of a German officer in the city. He smuggled a letter to Constantinople, managed to see that it was mailed to the American missionary headquarters in Boston and to make arrangements for receiving a small amount of money each month.

But each day more children wandered in from the mountains. The news of what Miss Jacobsen was doing spread; children almost dead of starvation and disease walked miles, to slip into the city by night. Boys and girls of every age, some who had managed to keep in fair health, others already beyond saving—each night they came until there were three thousand in the ruins.

There came the time when Miss Jacobsen must somehow get more help. It was impossible to get more money from America. And the secret family was increasing at the alarming rate of a hundred children a month.

"I realized that if we did not get more help we would

all die," Miss Jacobsen told me. "God gave me the thought and the courage to do what I did."

There was a new Turkish garrison commander in Harpoot, a man Miss Jacobsen had never met. But she had heard rumors that he was a kind man, not in sympathy with the massacre of Armenians. She went to the Turkish major.

"I told him I recognized him as a friend and that I had something to tell him that nobody—no other Turk—in the city knew."

It must have been an amazed Turk who then heard that a lone Danish nurse had been hiding over 3,000 children under the noses of a 5,000-man garrison! Miss Jacobsen told the soldier that she had no more food, must have help or her family would starve. He promised to think the matter over. In a few days he sent a message that Miss Jacobsen should see him.

The Turkish officer agreed to allow Miss Jacobsen to buy wheat from military stores, giving each child the same ration received by his soldiers. Having no money, she was to pay with what she calls "papers," or promissory notes. The officer had only one condition. Since many of his colleagues did not share his humanitarian views, she must still keep her family secret.

"But this was no problem now," Miss Jacobsen explained. "These many children never came out during the day, they had learned never to play, never to talk."

With the help of the Turkish officer, the children could be fed. The death rate dropped sharply and by June, 1919, there were 3,600 children in Maria Jacobsen's secret family.

Turkey was granted an armistice on October 30, 1918. But it was June 16, 1919, before outside help came to Har-

poot. On that day fifteen American Near East Relief workers arrived, with twenty-four big trucks loaded with food
and clothing.

Miss Jacobsen wrote her story for me and she ended it,
"There are many other things to tell but it would be too
long. The Turks could have killed me many times. But
God protected us and not one child was taken from me.
. . . I left Harpoot in September after the work had been
divided up among the fifteen Americans. But when I got
home to Denmark, I had forgotten how to smile and laugh.
. . . In the beginning I could not eat because of the lump
in my throat when I saw all the food. And it was especially
hard when I heard people complain of what they had
missed during the war. But in spite of the danger, the suffering, the sorrow and hardships, I thank the Lord for allowing me to help. I think, that counting all, even those
who died, there were about seven thousand children."

Maria Jacobsen did not give up her work with Armenian
children. She is now Superintendent of the Danish Bird's
Nest, a home for Armenian children at Djoubeil, Lebanon.
After World War I ended, the Armenians still alive were
taken out of Turkey and over 300,000 were settled in Lebanon and Syria. In the years that have passed thousands of
Armenians have gone to Russia, to live in the Armenian
Soviet Socialist Republic where 85 per cent of the population is Armenian. Others have gone to America. But there
still remain 150,000 in Lebanon and Syria.

The Danish Bird's Nest was started in 1922 with assistance from Near East Relief. Maria Jacobsen's sister Anna
was the Bird's Nest's first superintendent. Maria did not
arrive until 1931, and since that time she has directed the
work of the home.

Djoubeil, also known as Byblos, lies on the Mediterranean coast thirty-four kilometers north of Beirut. The town shares with Damascus the claim of being the oldest continually inhabited place in the world. It is a beautiful and fascinating place, literally cluttered with fallen columns, sarcophagi, carved cornices, blocks of classic masonry. There are remains of Roman temples and Phoenician temples. Gold, bronze, silver and copper coins of the Greco-Roman-Byzantine period are found throughout the town.

The Bird's Nest lies in the shadows of Djoubeil's most famous ruins, a Crusader castle built by the Barons of Giblet in 1109. There are 182 children living in this exotic spot, and 132 have American CCF sponsors. It is a terribly crowded Home, the buildings all needing repairs. There is neither place nor money for cottages. Children sleep in drafty dormitories, one building for girls having sixty beds in one room.

It is not usually possible for children to develop normally in such circumstances so that it is much to the credit of Maria and Anna Jacobsen that in spite of difficulties they have been able to do a remarkable job. Bird's Nest alumni do well in the outside world, include more than a hundred trained nurses working all through the Middle East and even in America.

One of the serious problems faced by the children is the tremendous heat of summer. Even though the Bird's Nest is within a stone's throw of the ocean, the heat is stifling. The home has been able to buy a plot of land on a mountainside three thousand feet in elevation. Each June the children move to the mountain and stay until September. The girls sleep in two wooden barracks, the boys on the ground among the trees.

The Bird's Nest is supported by the Lutheran Church in Denmark and Norway, by the Bible Lands Missions Society in England, by the Christian Children's Fund, by the gifts of its many alumni and other Armenians, especially those who have gotten to America. But it faces continual financial crises, has continual physical needs. In her 1955 report, Maria Jacobsen lists some of the pressing needs: a cistern for gathering rain water at Terzaya, the summer camp (the older boys now carry water nearly two miles); warm clothing for the children; toys for the younger boys and girls; 100 wool quilts; 100 wool mattresses, 200 bath towels, 200 face towels.

But the greatest need is for more and new buildings, for facilities to take in the many other children who desperately need help. The Reverend Olaf Passke, Bird's Nest chaplain, described for me in vivid terms the life that goes on in the Armenian slums of Beirut, whence most of the Bird's Nest children come. There is every type of corruption caused by the crowding of thousands of people into quarters not fit for human beings. Prostitution, widespread use of narcotics, a frightening incidence of tuberculosis— these are the causes of the broken homes that keep the Bird's Nest always filled.

And always there must be in the minds of the people the fact that they are truly without a country. Staunchly Christian, members of one of the earliest branches of the church, the people must live in a predominantly Moslem land. At the Bird's Nest they study in their native tongue. But they must also learn Arabic, must attempt to make themselves into good citizens of their involuntarily adopted land.

Yet the children of the Bird's Nest and of the Aindjar Settlement are among the brightest and most cheerful I have ever seen. I shall never forget a Sunday spent at Djoubeil. At the request of the children I was guest speaker at church. My remarks were interpreted in Armenian by Danish Olaf Passke. And my subject, at the request of the orphans, was the plight of the poor children in Korea.

10

Within the Arctic Circle

AT RIUTULA, a tiny village of orphans 210 miles north of the Arctic Circle in Finnish Lapland, I saw children playing a game that I believe is played elsewhere only by Korean children. There is no English word that adequately describes it. A board is placed across a log, or rocks, to form a short seesaw. A child stands on each end, and the object is for each child in turn to be thrown high in the air, feet together, returning to the end of the board so that his momentum makes the child at the other end also go high—sometimes six to nine feet up.

This is not the only resemblance one notes between Finland and the Far East. There may be no etymological connection, but there are words that sound almost identical in Finnish and Korean. Heard at a distance, Finnish has the singsong quality of some of South China's highly tonal dialects.

Historically there are also similarities, particularly between Finland and Korea. Both nations have suffered sudden communist aggression, both have areas occupied by an alien power.

With half again the area, Finland has only one sixth Korea's population. But the loss of life and the number of crippled and orphaned are proportionately far higher in Finland.

Each nation has suffered tremendous destruction and loss of territory but there is a great difference in result. The story of Korea is still one of tragedy and unsolved problems; that of Finland is a story of victory, of solution of problems that seemed impossible of solution.

To understand what has happened to Finland and its children, to appreciate what has been accomplished, it is necessary to review briefly the history of this little nation during the past fifteen-odd years.

Like Korea, Finland has been an independent nation for a short time. For several centuries ruled by the Swedes, then for almost a century by the Russian Czars, Finland became independent after World War I. On November 30, 1939, Finland was invaded by Soviet Russia. The Finns do not speak of this war as the Russo-Finnish war, do not generally mention the enemy by name. It is called simply "The Winter War." For a hundred days this tiny nation of less than four million population held off the Russian armies. But without aid it was inevitable that Finland would be defeated. With defeat came the loss of sixteen thousand square miles of territory, the creation of a large displaced population, thousands of widows and orphans.

For a very short time Finland was at peace. Then, under German pressure and unprovoked Russian bombing attacks, Finland became involved in World War II against Russia. In return for arms and munitions, the Finns allowed the Germans to move a large army into Lapland. The Finns meanwhile vigorously fought their recent invaders, driving the Russians out of all the territory ceded and threatening the important Arctic port of Murmansk.

For the Finns this was an uncomfortable and strange war, in which their nation was allied against America. It was a strange situation because although a member of the

Axis alliance, Finland was not actually at war with the United States, for to be at war with the United States would have been unthinkable to the Finns. And the situation became more difficult when America made clear that she would not welcome further Finnish advances toward Murmansk, the port into which thousands of tons of American aid were pouring.

Suddenly, in September, 1944, the situation became even more involved. Germany was on the brink of defeat. Russia forced Finland to come to terms, gave the Finns two weeks to clear the German army out of Finland.

The Finns again do not name the enemy, but speak of the terrible weeks of late 1944 as "The Destruction." There were over 100,000 German troops in Finland, concentrated in Lapland. As the Germans retreated they destroyed, burned, mined.

Lapland, covering 38,300 square miles, or almost one third of Finland, was literally burned to the ground. Methodically the Finns totted up the damage: 16,000 buildings destroyed; Rovaniemi, the capital of Lapland, and all other major towns, 100 per cent destroyed; 150,000 people driven out; 516 highway bridges, 218 railway bridges, all culverts destroyed; 8,000 cows, 26,000 sheep and 100,000 reindeer killed.

Not content with destroying all Lapland, the Germans mined the ruins. The wreckage of private homes, schools, churches and hospitals was strewn with mines. When the people returned after "The Destruction," thousands were killed or maimed by mines. For months people lived in dugouts, cellars, holes in the ground. Starvation and TB swept Lapland like a plague.

The total loss from these tragic events we in America have largely forgotten: 80,000 people killed, or one out of every fifty; 30,000 widows; 50,000 maimed and crippled in the military services plus 27,000 civilians. And the Winter War, the War of 1941-44, the Destruction, produced a total of 50,000 orphans—one orphan for every eighty people. In Korea there is one orphan for every 365 people.

Certainly no other nation in modern history has suffered such destruction. Even after peace came, the Finns were faced with tremendous problems other than the care of the wounded, the widowed, the orphaned. For eight years it was necessary for every Finn to pay 30 per cent of his earnings toward the tremendous reparations levied against the country by Russia.

"We did not think we could do it. And the Russians were sure we could never keep up the payments," a Finnish official told me. But by 1952 the last payment in goods had been made on the $226,500,000 reparations bill.

In the past decade 500,000 displaced people, or one eighth of the total population, have been resettled in new homes. Cities completely destroyed have been rebuilt. The children directly orphaned as a result of the Winter War and the Destruction have all been cared for in a remarkable program. The young were placed in orphanages while the Finnish Government sought to have them adopted by families which had lost their own children. At the age of sixteen every child who needed the help was placed in a vocational training school. The government provided food, free lodging, clothes, a tiny bit of spending money.

Already over thirty thousand orphaned children have graduated from the vocational training schools and are engaged in productive activity. The program reached its peak in 1954, and the number of boys and girls in the special vocational schools is now decreasing rapidly each year. Several thousand still remain in Finland's 207 orphanages, to move on at the age of sixteen to the training schools. These are the children who as babies or at two or three years of age lost their parents during the Destruction, or in the holocaust of exploding mines that ripped through Lapland in late 1944 and early 1945.

To understand the magnitude of this undertaking we must remember that while the Finns were taking care of their orphans and widows, they were also paying the $226,500,000 war indemnity to Russia and absorbing 500,-000 displaced persons. No other nation in modern times has accomplished so much with so little.

The visitor to Finland, knowing the history of the last fifteen years, cannot but be impressed. The job of reconstruction has progressed in all parts of the country. But it is in the province of Lapland, lying almost entirely within the Arctic Circle, that the most thrilling job has been done. It was to Lapland that I went, to visit the orphanages affiliated with the Christian Children's Fund and to see what the Finns are doing in child welfare.

It was Lapland that felt the full force of the Destruction. The physical reminders of 1944-45 are still seen, all along the "Ice Sea Highway" that leads straight north from Rovaniemi to the Arctic Ocean. There are still lonely ruins, stark chimneys where once was a lumberman's or farmer's home. There are many towns and villages with churches still not rebuilt.

And there are other results of the Destruction, apparent in the lives of the people. The fight against TB must still be waged. In 1950 five children a day contracted the disease and through the early '50's from 300 to 500 people died each year, 36 per cent of them children.

There has been an increase in mental illness, in alcoholism, in the number of illegitimate children. These are indirect effects of the wars and the Destruction, and are especially evident among the young men and women from age twenty-five to thirty-five.

These indirect results of war, of tension, of a difficult struggle for existence, create Lapland's present child welfare problem. There are 1,800 war orphans (the total population of Lapland is 180,000) in the vocational schools. There are 350 beds in eleven orphanages for the war orphans who are not yet in vocational schools and for the smaller children who are homeless or unwanted because of abandonment, mental illness of one or both parents, death of one or both parents from disease, and because of illegitimacy.

Three hundred and fifty children in eleven homes may not seem a large number for a population of 180,000 people. It is in fact large in proportion to population. For instance, Lapland has one eighth as many children in institutions as does my home state of Tennessee. But the population of Lapland is only one twentieth that of Tennessee.

And the problem of children in Lapland cannot be gauged by their numbers. The Finnish Government conceives of an orphanage as a receiving home, where children are cared for and restored to physical and mental health until foster parents can be found. Some children remain in the homes for years, but others move out in months or in two or three years. Thus there it a steady stream of new children and tiny babies entering each home every year.

Adoptions in Lapland itself are not common since the average family in this province is already large. In most villages 60 per cent of the population is under sixteen years of age; families of ten children are not uncommon. If Lapland orphans are to be adopted, it must be in South Finland or abroad.

My visit to Lapland took place in late April. It was already close to the season of the midnight sun, with only four hours of real darkness. But Lapland was still blanketed in deep snow, its myriad lakes and rushing rivers still frozen.

I was met at Rovaniemi's airport, one mile north of the Arctic Circle, by Reino Sarvola, Social Welfare Inspector for Lapland. I do not believe any American can have a complete visit to Lapland unless he has met Mr. Sarvola. Welfare expert, in charge of orphanages, homes for the aged, blind schools, Sarvola is also many other things. One of Lapland's best-known hunters and fishermen, an expert photographer and cameraman, graduate of law school and trained in animal husbandry, Sarvola is also Lapland's unofficial ski-master, with frequent ski trips of sixty miles in one day to his credit.

Reino Sarvola travels the "Ice Sea Highway" to the far north of Lapland once each month. He knows every twist and turn in the icy road, pushes his tiny Volkswagen at what at first is a terrifying speed. But it soon becomes apparent that Sarvola knows as few drivers do how to travel on snow and ice.

From Rovaniemi we took the highway 210 miles north of the Arctic Circle. The Finns are proud of their Circle; a sign in English, French and Finnish announces your passing of it, and a tiny log post office is kept open for visitors who want an Arctic Circle postmark. We went through Ivalo, largest city in the Far North, on past the thriving village of Inari to the shores of Lake Moddus.

The highway sweeps on to the north and the Norwegian border but we left the road at Lake Moddus. For my first orphanage stop was to be Riutula, claimed by the Finns to be the most northerly orphanage in the world. I see no reason to contest the claim. Riutula is the same latitude as the middle third of Greenland, farther north than any part of Alaska except the region around Point Barrow.

In winter the journey from the Ice Sea Highway to Riutula is made by *pulkka;* in summer by motorboat.

A pulkka is a tiny boatlike affair, six feet long, just wide enough for a man to sit with feet outstretched. To it is hitched a reindeer. If there is more than one pulkka in a party several are tied together in a line. It was thus that I started out across Lake Moddus, middle man in a three-unit pulkka train. Mr. Sarvola had his own beast and pulkka, traveling parallel to me and mine in order to take pictures.

The temperature hovered at zero, there was a biting wind across the lake. And reindeer travel cannot be described as comfortable, whatever the weather. A stream of snow flies from the reindeer's hoofs, directly into the face of the pulkka rider. The reindeer start off at a very fast clip, but on a somewhat unpredictable course. Gradually they slow down until they come to a halt, panting doglike. Then there is a great eating of snow until, refreshed, the animals start off without warning and with a tremendous jerk—perhaps toward the travelers' destination or just as likely toward some nice patch of lichen in the nearby forests.

Riutula, at the end of the pulkka trail, is one of the oldest orphanages in Finland. It was established in 1904 as a home for orphaned Lapp children and aged Lapps. Being far off the beaten track, it is among the handful of buildings in all Lapland that escaped during the Destruction.

Riutula is not a village. There is nothing there but the Lastenkoti (Children's Home) and a school. The nearest neighbors are a Lapp family living three miles away in the forest. It is a beautiful place, built amidst pines and birches on the shores of Lake Moddus where a rushing river flows south connecting it to innumerable other lakes. Except for the lake and the river, forests lie in every direction. Northward, they stretch to the Arctic Ocean ninety miles away.

I wondered why an orphanage was built in a place so remote, so difficult to supply. Reino Sarvola explained that when Riutula was founded in 1904 (the present main building was completed in 1907) it was on the mail trail that led from Kittila in Central Lapland to Petsamo, Finnish port on the Arctic Ocean. In those days the Ice Sea Highway had not been built, travel was either by boat and overland in the summer, or by ski and pulkka in the winter. The building of the highway in the '20's left Riutula in the backwash, a cluster of lonely red buildings against a background of deep forests.

Until the Christian Children's Fund gave money to extend a power line to the home in 1954, it had no electricity. Now it has the benefits of electric power, including a pump (which freezes each winter). It is also connected by phone with the village of Inari, nearly ten miles distant.

There are twenty-three children in Riutula, and a measure of their isolation is the fact that only three children have ever seen a movie. Once a week a traveling show comes to Inari.

One third of the children are Lapps, their oriental origin proclaimed by dark skin and hair and typically oriental features. Another third are of Lapp-Finnish mixture, or are from the tiny tribe of Skolt Lapps who once lived in the part of Finland bordering the Arctic Ocean and taken by Russia. The Skolt Lapps are Russian Orthodox in religion, have for centuries intermarried with Russians, frequently have typically oriental features but very blond hair. The remaining children are of pure Finnish blood.

There are children in Riutula from the age of four months to sixteen years. The manner in which they live, the problems they face, the reasons for their being in a Lastenkoti, are more or less typical of other homes and children in Lapland. Problems of food and medical attention are more difficult because of isolation. But otherwise Riutula is a typical Lapland children's home, where the children live close to nature, in old and poorly furnished buildings but in an atmosphere of love and security that cannot be matched by orphanages anywhere in the world.

The Finns in general, the Lapps in particular, are devoted to children. The Finnish Welfare officials believe it is of paramount importance to give orphaned children an extra sense of security, an extra amount of attention. Thus they strive to have no more than thirty children in each home, all living in one house. The main buildings are large, rambling structures and rarely do more than four children share the same sleeping quarters.

For each three children there is supposed to be *one trained attendant*. It is not always possible to keep this remarkable ratio, but six of the eleven homes in Lapland have managed to do so. All attendants are trained, and that is especially true of the superintendents.

Miss Elsa Kack, in charge at Riutula, has nearly a quarter of a century of experience with orphaned and unwanted children. Like all other superintendents she has taken a special two-year training course. Added to that is a six months' internship in a home.

I know of no orphanage in America able to keep a ratio of one attendant to three children; nor do I know of any which require such elaborate training for supervisory personnel. The results in Lapland are unusual. There is no feeling of being in an institution. At Riutula, as at all other homes I visited, there is an obvious warmth of relationship among the children and between children and attendants. There is shyness only among a few very young children. The others crowd about the visitor, delightfully curious and with heartwarming friendliness. The older children discuss their cases intelligently. Thus twelve-year-old Laila, queen bee of the Riutula children, abandoned by her father and mother, said simply, "This is my home now. I have all I want here."

Laila's father is a hunter in the nearby forests but has never come to see her. But if there are psychological problems in this bright and cheerful girl, they lie well hidden. Incidentally, even in remote Riutula there is psychological testing by trained welfare officials who visit the home each year.

Riutula has already graduated most of its true war orphans, the children who lost their parents during the Winter War and the Destruction. Most of the children in the home now are there because of the indirect results of these cataclysmic events or because of the harsh life of the Arctic. A half dozen have lost one or both parents because of TB or other illness. Miss Kack told me a typical story of a reindeer driver who passed by a forest hut seven kilometers from Riutula one winter day. At the window he noticed the faces of three children, pale and frightened. He stopped. Inside the little house he found the parents dead and three other children dead. All had been stricken by influenza, and the three remaining small children had been too frightened to go for help through the deep snow.

Frequently a Lapp hunter or fisherman, living deep in the forest, waits too long to take an expectant mother to the nearest midwife. Suddenly her time comes, and they must start out through the darkness by reindeer pulkka for a village twenty or forty miles away. Scores of children have lost their mothers because of childbirth deep in the forests at forty degrees below zero.

However, such events do not always end in tragedy. Reino Sarvola tells the story of a Lapp who started forth with his wife for a midwife twenty miles away. Halfway to his destination he saw fresh bear tracks. A bear would mean a tremendous amount to the family, in fresh meat and hide. The course seemed obvious: leave the wife in the pulkka, well covered with blankets, while the husband went forth on skis after the bear.

Many hours later the hunter returned, successful in his bear hunt, but suddenly remorseful about his wife. But he found her squatted by a roaring fire, baby safely arrived.

It was at Riutula that I first began to realize another indirect effect of war, evacuation, and destruction. Several children were in the home because one or both parents had cracked up mentally in the post-Destruction period. In other homes I found as many as five out of thirty children institutionalized for that reason. Coupled with mental illness is an alarming increase in chronic alcoholism and illegitimacy.

Reino Sarvola believes all these are results of the multiple strains under which the people of Lapland have lived for the past fifteen years. And he also believes that the situation is improving now that the worst is over, now that a gleaming new Lapland has risen from the ashes of the Destruction.

The Lapps have had a particularly difficult time. They are a Mongolian people, used to a free life of hunting, fishing, raising reindeer. During the Destruction the Lapps were evacuated to the cities of South Finland and Sweden. They had a difficult time adjusting to life away from their beloved rivers and forests. But they have come back home and their worst days are over. There are 2,500 Lapps in Finnish Lapland now, more than at any time in the memory of man. The Lapp is definitely not a vanishing race.

The children at Riutula have what for us would be an exotic diet. Reindeer meat is on the menu at least once a day all through the fall and winter. During this season the orphanage requires two animals every week. Then in late May when the lakes and rivers open, trout, salmon, grayling and delicious white fish replace reindeer meat. The children fish through the ice during the winter but when the ice is gone they use nets, catching enough fish to feed the orphanage each day. There are cows and plenty of fresh milk. And a small vegetable garden helps although green vegetables are always scarce.

But Riutula and all other Lapland homes are faced with financial problems. It costs from 450 to 485 Finnish marks per day to care for each child. This is equivalent to $1.40 a day or $42 a month. The Finnish Government provides 65 marks daily subsidy for babies and 55 for older children. The rest of the money comes from sponsoring organizations and, in the case of eight homes and 185 children, from American sponsors of children through the Christian Children's Fund.

Only two of the eleven Lapland homes are government institutions, financed by county government. Riutula is sponsored by the Finnish YWCA; other homes by local charitable organizations or by the General Mannerheim

Child Welfare League, founded by Finland's most famous and beloved general.

The great need at Riutula, and all the other homes, is one that could be easily filled by Americans. Winter closes in on Lapland in October, to stay until early May. During all this time there is an average of three feet of snow on the ground and temperatures frequently drop to forty degrees below zero. The children need warm clothes, coats, jackets, wool shirts and slacks for the older boys and girls, snowsuits for the toddlers. The child whose American CCF sponsor has sent warm clothing is very proud. At the Sodankyla Home fifty miles north of Rovaniemi I was met by a talkative four-year-old who seemed to have an urgent message to impart. She wished to inform me that the secondhand zippered coat she was about to put on had just come from her "friends in America."

At Riutula and at the other homes there are also other specific needs, things that they cannot purchase because of their limited funds. During the late spring and summer, travel to and from Riutula is by boat, so the Home needs a powerful outboard motor. At least two more boats are needed for the young fishermen who must go out on the lake and cast their nets for the Home each day. Sport fishing tackle—casting rods, fly rods, reels, flies, spoons and plugs: what happiness $50 worth of such equipment could bring to a dozen boys and girls living on the lonely shores of Lake Moddus!

I have written of Riutula in detail because it is unique in its isolation. But the problems faced there are in varying degrees faced in the other homes. In all the homes the children become expert skiers, fishermen, hunters. They become onlookers first, participants later, in the great social events of Lapland: the annual reindeer roundups in which thousands of these neither wild nor tame animals are corralled and lassoed so that ownership tags may be placed on their ears. There are 160,000 reindeer in Lapland, owned by members of 8,000 families. Under Finnish law the father, mother, and each child may own reindeer, and each has a registered earmark. There are now 16,000 earmarks in use.

While Riutula is the only home reached by reindeer pulkka, others are hardly in urban surroundings. The wonderful one at Meltaus is reached by crossing the Ounas River. During the winter the crossing is by ice, in summer by boat. For two weeks in the fall and two weeks in the spring Meltaus is marooned while the ice freezes hard or breaks enough to permit passage of boats.

Rovaniemi, Lapland's capital city, has only 15,000 population. Ivalo, main trade center in the far north, boasts 1,500. But wherever the homes may be, the children have not only excellent care but excellent schooling. Finnish law provides that there must be schools within reach of every school-age child. After the Destruction it was the schools that were rebuilt first. The result is that Finland has a literacy rate of 99 per cent, highest in the world.

Riutula, Meltaus, Sodankyla, Posio, Kittila, Salla—these homes are all of a pattern, the buildings frequently old, but everywhere a spirit of warmth reaches out from the moment the visitor steps in the door. After visiting these homes, I was in for still another surprise at Kemijarvi, my last stop.

Reino Sarvola gave me no warning of what to expect. I presumed that I would see a home similar to those already visited in eight hundred miles of travel over snowy roads, iced-in rivers and lakes. But the Kemijarvi Lastenkoti is something else, Reino Sarvola's dream of the future. A county-operated institution, this home is Finland's model. I doubt if there is anything like it elsewhere in the world.

Kemijarvi Lastenkoti stands on a spruce-covered knoll overlooking a river and lake. When I gasped at the beauty of the building, Sarvola said, "Ugly buildings cost just as much as beautiful buildings in the long run." And then he explained its marvels, every detail planned for children: wash basins are at different heights for various ages; children's furniture, including chairs, beds and lockers, of a half dozen sizes. Everywhere there are bright colors, picture windows looking out over the forests and river. The walls are paneled in bright Lapland wood.

Kemijarvi does not look like a children's home. It could easily be mistaken for a swank country club. Kemijarvi has bathtubs in addition to the traditional Finnish *sauna*, or steam bath. The nursery for the babies and toddlers is equipped with its own kitchen. There are refrigerators, electric stoves, washing machines. Built on three levels, the home has special playrooms for boys and girls, a guest room for visitors, spacious rooms for the staff.

Reino Sarvola is proud of his dream orphanage for a number of reasons. Kemijarvi lies not far from the Russian border, in an area fought over for months. Along roads nearby I saw the jagged remains of tank traps, vast areas completely deforested by shell fire. The nearby city was utterly destroyed. But when Mr. Sarvola explained to the county authorities that he would like to build an orphanage that would be a model for other counties, the men and women who only a few years ago had been destitute refugees agreed. With local financing, this children's paradise came into being.

Reino Sarvola is a man of many enthusiasms. Trout and salmon fishing, skiing, hunting black cock in the forests—

these are the things he likes to talk of. But it is when he explains about Kemijarvi that his face lights up, that his enthusiasm reaches its height.

"If children are to be happy, we must have trained people who have time for them. That means we must have at least one attendant per three children and I would prefer even more. And we must also have buildings constructed *for* children, easily maintained so that the staff does not have to spend all its time on housekeeping chores. We have tried to build here the home of the future, a home where unfortunate and unwanted children can find themselves."

Few children in the world have faced more tragic times than many of those I saw in Lapland's Lastenkoti. There was lovely little Helena, age three, hugging the doll sent by her American sponsor. Helena's family fled from the Petsamo area when it was seized by Russia, and settled near Ivalo. A Finnish Health Sister found Helena and eight brothers and sisters sleeping in hay, in a house without beds or blankets. Abandoned by the father, the mother and family were destitute.

At Kittila I played with Markku, aged four, Perjo, aged five and Kirrte, three, illegitimate children found abandoned and starving. At Meltaus there was bright Aatu Seppala whose parents were killed in the Destruction and who contracted TB. The local sanatorium was burned by the Germans and Aatu was given a special room, special diet and nursed back to health.

At Riutula there were five beautiful Finnish and Lapp girls whom I photographed with newborn lambs. Laila, Anni, Hilja, Inga and Terttu are lovely children glowing with health and happiness, all sponsored by Americans living in such diverse places as San Antonio, Washington, D.C., Mt. Dora, Florida, Waverly, Illinois.

I had the pleasure at Riutula of personally delivering a sponsor's letter to ten-year-old Karllo Valkonen, of watching him read it and of taking his answer to the outside world for mailing. I heard, at several homes, of the growing number of American sponsors who are personally visiting their children, women like Mrs. Dorothy Deane Scattergood of Albion, Michigan, who visited her eight-year-old Jaakko at Meltaus. Mrs. Scattergood had a broken leg at the time, hobbled on crutches. But she drove the long bumpy miles from Rovaniemi and crossed the roaring Oanus River to Meltaus to stay for three days.

But I will also not forget five-year-old Oili K., a girl born with inoperable cataracts on both eyes. Oili's parents broke under the stress and tensions of Finland's wars and destruction. She has been at the Salla Home since she was two years old, but is merely a number to her American sponsor—adoption number 10692, the only sponsored child at Salla who has never received a letter, never received a package.

When I visited Salla, Oili knew from the excitement and talk that a visitor from America had arrived. She rushed to me, hugging my legs, asking, "Are you my sponsor?"

Oili has been carefully examined by doctors. There is no hope for any sight in one eye, hope for only fractional vision in the other. After two more years at Salla, she will go into a school for the blind to be educated and trained for work the blind can perform.

Oili's problem will be solved as well as the problem of any blind child can be solved. It will be handled intelligently and with compassion, for every unfortunate child in Finland is important to the Finns. This remarkable people have been able to solve all but one of the problems rising from the Winter War and the Destruction.

Thousands of Finns and Lapps took refuge in Sweden during these events. Over twenty thousand children were sent to Sweden for safety. In Sweden the children were given loving care by their temporary Swedish foster parents. Sweden is a land of great prosperity compared to Finland. The Swedes gave the children things they had never had in Finland, lavished gifts on them.

When the wars ended, when the Finns began to dig out from the debris of the Destruction, they wanted their children. But many of the younger children who had gone to Sweden during the Winter War or the early days of the war of 1941-44 had forgotten their Finnish parents, could no longer speak Finnish. Many who did return to Finland were desperately unhappy, unable to adapt themselves to the rough life of a nation forced to rebuild its cities and villages. In many cases, also, Swedish foster parents had learned to love the children, were unwilling to give them up.

Today, twelve years after peace came to Finland, there are still ten thousand Finnish children in Sweden. In some cases the governments have forced children to return to their parents, but the results have not been good. And so ten thousand Finnish children will remain in a foreign land, their own parents still living and but a few hundred miles away. Reluctantly but wisely, the Finnish Government has decided that it will not force these children to return to the land of their birth.

11

Children of Western Europe

ONE who has spent a lifetime in Asia becomes somewhat hardened to misery and starvation. The sight of walking dead, of leprous beggars and ragged children is commonplace. Slums and human squalor are taken for granted in Hong Kong, Calcutta or Seoul. But the commonplace becomes shocking when seen among people of our own color or cultural background. While traveling around the world, the first shock came to me in Beirut, to find in that beautiful city on the sea areas where thousands of men and women exist in squalor that matches anything that is found in the Far East.

And in Europe the traveler who knows where to look can find the same misery, areas where people exist animal-like, with little hope of anything better. There are refugee camps and slums, and slums produced by the pressure of overpopulation and underemployment. Always the birth rate is high, and the main sufferers are the children.

Unfortunately the problems of unwanted children in Europe have been beclouded by a curious American tendency to write and talk about the illegitimate children of our own soldiers. In April, 1956, a leading American home magazine carried a feature entitled "The Sins of the Fathers." A lead paragraph stated, "All through Europe

159

and the Orient today there are 400,000 little boys and girls who know only one fact about their daddies: that they are Americans."

There is no basis for this statement, just as there was no basis for a feature story in another magazine accusing Americans of fathering 110,000 children in Japan when actually the number is nearer 7,000. The 400,000 war and occupation babies in the world include those fathered by Germans, Russians, French, British and Japanese. They are in need, and many are in institutions. But it is probable that less than half have American fathers. The continued effort to castigate ourselves diverts attention from other children who also need assistance and understanding.

To tell in part the story of Western Europe's orphaned children I write of three people, living in widely separated cities, and of the work they are doing. One is a Protestant minister in Catholic Italy; one is a refugee woman in Paris; the third is a man who gave up a dream of practicing medicine for a new dream that has been made into remarkable reality.

I begin with a story of Italy and the lovely city of Naples. The average American tourist will not visit its Mercato district. Lying along the waterfront, this area was heavily bombed during World War II. And I have seen no city in Japan where less effort has been made to rebuild. The scars of war, long healed in most cities, are still startlingly fresh in Naples.

There are buildings in the Mercato district, also in the nearby Granili district, where the upper floors were smashed and gutted and their shells remain with expanses of blank windows, crazily leaning walls. Thousands of people live in the basements. Nearby are other areas where the bombed ruins have in part been cleared away. Here people also live, in jerry-built houses where blankets serve as window coverings, or in fragments of buildings made habitable by coverings of bits of wood and salvaged tin.

It was raining the day I drove through the Mercato district, and the spaces between houses, the open areas that divided ruins from ruins, were a sea of mud. There are no access roads as such, merely openings where buildings once stood. Everywhere there are small children, a remarkable number, all filthy, all dressed in rags. Among the smaller children are also scores of older boys, hard-eyed and wary, who make their living or contribute to the family welfare by a variety of activities. There are pimps who procure for their teenage sisters, purse-snatchers, petty thieves, others who specialize in cigarette-butt collecting (current price somewhat over $1 per pound of butts). Collectively these children of the slums are known as *scugnizzi*, or the "spinning tops." And if there be enough money involved, the scugnizzi frequently extend their activities beyond petty larceny. Muggings, even murder, are not uncommon.

These are not children of American GI's. They are largely products of economic depression, of a city where a minimum of 40,000 lire a month is required to live, while the average earnings are 22,000 lire. Ten thousand people live in the bombed-out buildings of the Mercato district, one third of them unemployed. There are few men living along the waterfront who can remember when conditions were different. Even before the bombings depressions were so frequent that they were the rule rather than the exception.

A few blocks beyond the Mercato district in an area known as Portici there is an unexpected oasis of green trees and laughter, an area that teems with adequately dressed and happy children whose every action is in sharp contrast to those of the scugnizzi who prowl the streets nearby.

A sign proclaims that the visitor has entered the Casa Materna, one of Italy's largest children's homes, an institution which came into being a half century ago purely by accident.

In 1905 Riccardo Santi was among the very few Protestant ministers in all Italy. It was on June 12th of that year that Pastor Santi laid the foundation for today's Casa Materna. It was his birthday, and Signora Santi asked her husband to leave the house for an hour or so while she prepared a special birthday dinner.

Pastor Santi wandered aimlessly about the waterfront streets. At a street corner he noticed two small children, a boy and a girl, vainly trying to sell matches. The children were shivering, not from cold but from misery and hunger. On an impulse, Pastor Santi asked why they did not go home to supper. The older child replied, "We have no home. We live in the streets."

Riccardo Santi took the children home to share his birthday dinner. After dinner the sleepy waifs were put to bed with the two Santi children. They spent the rest of the week with the Santi family, for niether Pastor Santi nor his wife had the heart to put out two children who had suddenly found heaven.

The salary of a Methodist minister in Italy is not large, even today. A half century ago it was much smaller, and two extra mouths to feed presented a problem. The following Sunday Pastor Santi shared the problem with his congregation. That afternoon extra beds, clothing, donations of food were brought to the house. Pastor Santi did not know it, but the Casa Materna had been established. Good news travels fast among children of the streets, and soon other waifs were knocking on the Santi door.

It soon became necessary to rent a building for the growing family. As the years passed the growth continued and it was necessary to make several moves, to establish a school, open not only to the orphan children but to others who could not pay tuition fees.

These are typical case histories of children now in the home: Antonietta, thought to be nine years old, was found in a house of prostitution when it was raided by American Military Police. No one knows when she was born, nor the identity of her parents. The little girl had become a sort of mascot in the house of ill fame. Or there is Vincenzo, now fifteen years old but just completing the first grade. He was found wandering about the streets of Portici, unable to talk but able to sing a little tune made up of the words "Za-za, Za-za," repeated over and over again. Inevitably Za-Za became his name. The boy has spent two years in a TB hospital, in 1956 had operations on both ears. He has learned to talk, is slowly recovering from the mistreatment that almost crippled him, mentally and physically. Za-Za's uncle appeared at Casa Materna two years ago and although unwilling to take the boy, or even help him, at least provided him with a name. Carlo Corridori has no family whatsoever. His father was killed during the war, all his other relatives were killed in a gas explosion. Carlo was found alive and unhurt in the ruins.

Today's Casa Materna is located in the former palace of the Prince of Monaco (not Prince Rainier; perhaps his father or grandfather). Covering seven acres, with three large buildings and a beach looking out to the Isle of Capri, it is truly an oasis in the midst of human desert.

Unemployment is the great problem of Naples but, as is true in so many places, there are jobs for those who are skilled with their hands. In 1948 an excellent carpentry shop was built and later a printing shop added. The Santis hope to develop other vocational training programs for their boys; already there are courses in dressmaking and domestic science for the girls.

In 1956 there were 285 orphaned and abandoned children at Casa Materna; another 210 day students were attending the school. Since the first two children joined the Santi family in 1905, Casa Materna has graduated 8,177 boys and girls. Even by American standards many of these children of the streets have become successful. One of the most beloved Methodist ministers in Italy is a Casa Materna graduate who had been found abandoned in the streets. Two Greek children brought to the home by the Salvation Army are now successful dentists in America. The three Cecere brothers, abandoned by their parents, have become, respectively, a pilot in the port of Naples, a major in the Italian Army, a successful manufacturer of costume jewelry in America.

Director Fabrio Santi is justifiably proud of these graduates, also of boys like Luigi, graduated in 1955 and now chief mechanic in Naples' Coca-Cola plant. As has been proved by the Schnellers in the Middle East and by Bill Henry among the outcastes of India, jobs are available for boys and girls who are trained, who have learned to use their hands as well as their heads. Few of Casa Materna's graduates become rich, but there are also very few of them among Naples' 100,000 chronically unemployed.

The Casa Materna receives $2,000 annually from the Methodist Board of World Missions, $12,000 from Americans who have sponsored children through the Christian Children's Fund. But the Home's main support comes through the efforts of the Santi family. Riccardo Santi is now eighty years old, but he is ably assisted by two sons, one of whom, Fabrio, has become Director. Another son, Dr. Immanuel Santi of White Plains, New York, is also able to help in the never-ceasing battle to raise funds. In 1956 Director Fabrio Santi and the Casa Materna choir visited America (on borrowed money) and were able to raise a considerable sum over expenses for the many improvements and the expansion the Santis are planning.

But the cost of living is ever on an upward spiral in Italy. The price of sugar is up 35 per cent over last year, cooking oil that cost 350 lire a liter two years ago now costs 900 lire. It is not easy to care for 285 orphans, to run a school, to give first-rate vocational training to older boys and girls on faith alone! One of Director Fabrio Santi's hopes is that some day all of the 285 orphans will be sponsored by Americans, for then the yearly gap between income and expenses could be closed.

As bad as are conditions in Naples, they could be much worse had not the Santi family pioneered in child welfare work, in developing educational facilities. When the Casa Materna was founded there were three orphanages and two schools in the area. Today, largely because of the Casa Materna influence, there are eighteen children's homes and thirty-two schools in the Portici area of Naples.

From the Casa Materna beach there is a clear view of the Isle of Capri. I could not but wonder at the changes and improvements that could be made if each American who goes to Capri could also visit the waterfront slums, could see the miracle of Casa Materna, an island of hope rising from the squalor of streets infested with scugnizzi. The Casa Materna has saved scores of boys from becoming "spinning tops," scores of girls from prostitution. If each American tourist could spend one tenth of his Capri vacation expenses on Casa Materna, on the several excellent Catholic institutions of a similar nature, how much more could the ranks of the scugnizzi be reduced!

Paris, although it enjoys much greater economic stability than Naples, has its slums, its problems of young hoodlums. But I write a different story of Paris, one involving a small refugee group. There are forty thousand Russians in Paris, men and women who escaped after the communists took over their country. Intensely anticommunist, generally devoutly religious, the refugee Russians have but one dream, to live so that one day they may have a part in re-creating their country.

But while they dream, they have problems of making a living, of keeping their families together. Extreme poverty has been the lot of many, and poverty's handmaidens— disease, alcoholism, crime—have taken their toll.

Fifteen miles south of Paris there is a home for Russian orphans. Called the Foyer des Enfants, it is located in an ancient castle which legend says was built originally by Queen Anne, a Russian, in the thirteenth century. Through the centuries the castle has been many other things: a monastery, a grain mill, a refuge for a rich expatriate American woman. Today it is the home of eighty-six Russian or part-Russian children, supervised by one of the most remarkable people I have every known.

Miss Sophia Zernoff is herself a refugee. Her father was a prominent Moscow doctor during the '20's. Both father and brother were in the White Russian army. The Reds placed a price upon their heads. The Zernoffs escaped to the Caucasus Mountains and walked from there through the mountains into Georgia.

With the help of a British diplomat the family was smuggled to Constantinople. From Turkey the trail led on into Yugoslavia where the Zernoff family settled down to live, and the children were educated. In 1935 another move was necessary, and the family went to Paris.

"We lost everything we possessed during the Revolution," Miss Zernoff told me, "but we found God, and now we are not afraid of anything." The story of the Foyer des Enfants is an indication of Miss Zernoff's faith. The home is entirely her creation, developed in the face of tremendous odds.

Miss Zernoff found her castle in 1939, borrowed money for an initial payment. But 3,000,000 francs were needed to close the deal. She went to four different banks, none of which would lend additional money on a run-down property already heavily encumbered.

"We had a day or so left if we were to keep the place," Miss Zernoff told me. "I dared to ask God for help. In His name I asked for three million francs. The next morning I went to my office. I found a letter from a Dutchman, in charge of a Dutch Youth Movement. There was a check for three million francs—not two million nor four million, but exactly what I had asked for."

With the unexpected help of her Dutch giver, Miss Zernoff was able to make the castle livable, to create a home inhabited by what the French Government's Director of Social Assistance calls "the happiest children in France."

I met these happy children on a rainy January day,

talked to many of them through a Russian Orthodox priest who visits the home regularly to instruct the children in the Russian faith.

Typical is the story of three boys, Joseph, age twelve; Michael, ten; Alexis, seven. The mother is Russian, the father French. The father, when he was a prisoner of war in Germany, met a Russian woman there and she bore him the three boys. After the war the French soldier brought the family to Paris, but immediately abandoned them for his French wife, about whom the Russian wife had never been told. The woman broke under the strain and is now in a mental institution. Technically, of course, these boys are not orphans. Their father is alive, somewhere in France. Their mother is alive, but in an institution.

Or there is the story of a girl, age fifteen, whose name Miss Zernoff asked me not to use. The family lived in a sex hotel in the Paris slums. The father acted as pimp for the mother. When the girl was six years old she witnessed a tragic event. Her father brought in a customer who was drunk. The mother, in a fit of fury, killed the father with a butcher knife. After a term in prison the woman was released; now she is the mistress of another man.

But perhaps most interesting is the story of another little girl, eight-year-old Tatiana. Tatiana's mother was fifteen years old when taken by the Germans for forced labor. She was sent to Czechoslovakia where she escaped to become active in the underground. Little more than a girl herself, the woman was instrumental in saving the lives of numerous French prisoners, led groups of them across the Czech border. The prisoners brought her back to Paris with them. One prisoner, a young doctor, promised to marry her. But after Tatiana was born the Frenchman disappeared, leaving neither money nor address.

The prisoners saved by Tatiana's mother had all expressed heartfelt gratitude, had all promised to help. They never did, and Tatiana was brought to the Foyer des Enfants. But the story did not end.

Tatiana's mother, still young and attractive, was befriended by an Indo-Chinese student in a Paris university. He too talked of marriage; but after the birth of a little boy, he too walked out. Now little brown-skinned Sarter is with his sister at the home. And the mother, still young, still pretty, may quite possibly add another child to Miss Zernoff's family.

"These children are innocent," Miss Zernoff says, "and I believe that often the parents are innocent too, victims of the cruel epoch in which it was given us to live."

Most of the children at the Foyer des Enfants are, like Tatiana and her half-brother, part Russian. There are two part-American children whose father deserted their Russian mother. There are children like seven-year-old André, parents both Russian but the father with TB, the mother mentally ill.

As has so often been the case, the Christian Children's Fund found Miss Zernoff purely by accident. Her brother was traveling in India, happened to visit the Malabar Coast, happened to learn of the CCF's Alwaye Settlement. He wrote his sister about the work being done there; she in turn wrote Dr. Clarke. Two years ago the Foyer des Enfants became affiliated with CCF, now receives a $6,000 annual subsidy.

With CCF help, with the unexpected Dutch gift, with help received from the French Government, Miss Zernoff has created a paradise for children in her old castle. One building is appropriately known as the Dutch Dormitory. The stables have been made into a boys' dormitory. But

Miss Zernoff's dream is to be able to buy an adjacent tract of wooded ground so that she can develop a playground and also have a place to grow vegetables.

It is expensive to care for children in France, and each month brings a new financial crisis with an average deficit of $800. Sometimes the deficit is made up by borrowing, sometimes by an unexpected gift; sometimes several months' deficits pile up before help comes from some source.

I had a small part to play in such unexpected help. Miss Zernoff told me that one of the home's greatest needs was a car. Her own ancient vehicle, a typical small European make with 200,000 miles on its speedometer, seldom made the trip from Paris without a breakdown. I mentioned this fact to Dr. Clarke, and Miss Zernoff now has a new car.

Miss Zernoff has a constant problem in finding and keeping good teachers. Her dream, and that of the committee which helps supervise the home, is to train young Russians who may some day have a part in the rehabilitation of their homeland. Teachers and staff members must therefore be bilingual in Russian and French. The home is able to pay a salary of 15,000 francs a month ($40), and only men and women who also share in Miss Zernoff's dream are willing to work at this salary.

Since its beginnings in 1939, the Foyer des Enfants has graduated a remarkable fifteen hundred boys and girls. Nearly all graduates have good positions; many have gone to America, Canada, Latin America. More and more of the boys are finding excellent positions with the French Government, which needs men who can speak Russian. One recent graduate is now the top Russian interpreter in the French Army.

Miss Zernoff's dream of the day when her boys and girls will return to Russia may never be realized. But she is doing a remarkable service for the Russian refugee population of France. Remembering her statement that "We lost everything during the Revolution but we found God and now we are not afraid of anything," I would guess that her more immediate dreams will be realized. These are to find, somewhere, financial help to take care of the $800 monthly deficit; to find another $2,000 for repairs badly needed by a castle that has seen much better days; to secure the further financial help which would enable the Foyer des Enfants to take in the twenty-five to thirty children who are always on the waiting list.

For every Russian refugee there are thousands of refugees and displaced persons from the other nations of Eastern Europe. Many families have found homes in Europe, even in America. But everywhere there are others who are still homeless, who live in bleak refugee camps, losing each month a bit of the faith that made possible their escapes from communist tyranny. Of course these populations of displaced and dispirited people produce their annual crop of unwanted, abandoned and orphan children.

The valley of the Upper Inn River in the Austrian Alps has a population of some thirty thousand DP's. A few of the camps can be seen from the railroad that runs from Zurich to Innsbruck. And also there can be seen from the railroad, although few tourists would know it, a remarkable effort to help the many children of post-war Europe who are in need of help.

Two miles from the tracks, on a hillside high above the Tyrolean town of Imst, there is a children's village—the

SOS Kinderdorf, it is called. It is a small town in itself, with fifteen two-story cottages, each with nine or ten children and a house mother. Physically, the only children's home I have seen elsewhere that can compare to the SOS Kinderdorf is Reino Sarvola's model home at Kemijarvi, Lapland.

The children's village in the Alps was founded by Dr. Hermann Gmeiner. My college German has long since receded into some inner recess of my brain, and Dr. Gmeiner knows little English. I cannot say, therefore, whether or not his dream for children is based on a deep religious faith like Miss Zernoff's. I do know that Dr. Gmeiner has a tremendous faith in his fellow man, in the willingness of people to help those who are less fortunate.

The SOS Kinderdorf has no official church connections or assistance, no government help, receives from the Christian Children's Fund only $2,000 annually. It is made possible by 240,000 individuals, mostly in Austria, who belong to the Children's Village Societies. Monthly dues are one schilling, a little less than four cents. In addition, industries and business firms throughout Austria, even in West Germany, have contributed to building and furnishing.

Dr. Gmeiner established the Children's Village at Imst in 1949 and the first cottage was completed the next year. There are now fifteen cottages, two more are under construction. As the children graduate from the Children's Village they are moved to Innsbruck, where they live in an SOS dormitory and become apprentice workers in business establishments.

The need among the displaced persons and the occupation children is so great that Dr. Gmeiner soon began planning other Children's Villages. A small Kinderdorf is already completed and in operation at Linz. During the summer of 1956 ten cottages were completed at the new Village at Altmünster. Children's Village number four is in the planning stage and will be built near Vienna. Number five is being planned near the town of Kärnten.

The Children's Village idea is catching on elsewhere in Europe. There is one in Switzerland, one in West Germany, one in France. In each case the pattern is the same. The cottages are well built and furnished, in beautiful surroundings. The children receive individual attention in small "family groups." Financial support comes from local citizens and business firms.

There are 136 children at the Imst Children's Village. Twenty are American GI children. One of the most lovable is a dark-skinned three-year-old named Andreá, the illegitimate child of an Indian student at a Vienna University. The Austrian mother was left with Andreá when the student returned to India.

But most of the children are typical products of Europe's vast population of refugees and displaced persons. There are children from Hungary, Rumania, Czechoslovakia, Yugoslavia, East Germany. Dr. Gmeiner had a number of his children prepare their stories for me, and I cite some that are typical:

I was born on November 27, 1943, in Hungary. At that time the war was on and my father and brother went into the army. My sister had already died, there was only my mother and I, and after the war we were forced to flee. At a rest period during our escape my mother became sick because it was very cold. The journey continued for a long time until we came to a town called Kitzbühel. There were other fugitives from our country, but they went on to West Germany seeking new homes. Some people took my mother to a hospital. I also was taken to the hospital because we did not know anyone in Austria who would take me in. After a short time my mother died, and I had to stay on at the hospital for a long time. One day an elderly lady was brought to the hospital. She was very ill for a time but recovered. She heard that I was an orphan, and she took me in. But soon she became ill again and died. Then for a while I stayed with the lady's daughter. But soon she did not want me any more. Now nobody wanted me any more. It was then that I was brought to the Children's Village, and now things go very well for me.

So the stories go. "I was three years old when my mother died. My father did not like me and gave me away. When nobody wanted me any more, he gave me to the Children's Village." Or, "My father was killed during the war. One day my mother went for a walk. At night she did not return. For several days we searched for her, and one day we found her lying dead on the bank of a brook. There was no one to care for me, and I came to the Children's Village."

When all five of Dr. Hermann Gmeiner's SOS Kinderdorfs are completed, nearly five hundred such children will find a home. The story of these Children's Villages in the Alps is an inspiring one, because it typifies the best that is in Western Europe, the willingness and the ability of men and women to solve their problems with a minimum of outside help. Dr. Gmeiner's dream villages are in a very real sense international children's homes to which the sick and weary, the unwanted of a half dozen nationalities can come for help.

In the words of Dr. Gmeiner, included in a little booklet describing his Kinderdorfs, "Here children who never had security or a sense of belonging can find love and understanding, regardless of their nationality or former back-ground. We try to give them confidence in themselves and their fellow men, to teach them trust and respect for their immediate cottage 'family.' All this is in preparation for a normal life later on, when they will leave the villages and can become good citizens able to take on the normal responsibilities of adult life without trouble."

The Children's Villages in the Alps have not been in existence long enough to produce an imposing number of graduates. Most of the children are products of the dislocation that followed World War II; many are under twelve years in age. But if beautiful surroundings, superbly equipped homes, excellent family relationships produce well-balanced adults, the years ahead will see many success stories result from Hermann Gmeiner's dream.

12

Susie Skinner

IT WAS a routine flight, but the Northwest Orient Airlines plane was overdue. The runways of Seattle's international airport were covered by fog that blew in from Puget Sound; the plane circled overhead awaiting a break in the overcast.

It was early morning of an October day in 1954. The usual crowd awaited arrival of the flight: wives of businessmen, dependents of U.S. Army and Navy personnel in the Far East, a handful of Chinese and Japanese. Clustered near the Customs Office was a tense group, a family of seven, including grandfather, parents and four children. With them were newspapermen, airlines officials, newsreel cameramen.

Shortly after nine o'clock the plane landed, taxied to the ramp. While flash bulbs popped and cameras whirred, the plane door opened and a tiny seven-year-old Chinese girl appeared. Dressed in red silk padded coat and trousers, she held tightly to the stewardess's hand.

"Take her in your arms," said Robert Barr of the Seattle *Times*. Dr. Lawrence Skinner stepped forward, picked the little girl up. Then Dr. J. E. Skinner, father of Lawrence Skinner, spoke to the little girl.

"Remember me, Susie?" he asked.

There was no sign of recognition. There was no fear, only an air of detachment as the little girl watched the antics of cameramen and officials. The official U.S. Customs interpreter talked rapidly to her in the Cantonese dialect. She calmly ignored the Chinese.

As the group entered the terminal building the Skinner children crowded about. Seven-year-old Jean jumped about as though possessed; twelve-year-old Dave managed an air of detachment; Jim, seventeen, had contrived against orders to be on the runway. And sixteen-year-old Sarah wiped away a tear. It was only when she saw the Skinner children that Susie, seven-year-old waif from Hong Kong, relaxed and flashed a big smile. Having exchanged pictures and letters for months they were, after all, old friends.

Newspapers throughtout America carried stories of the arrival of Tak Oi Shi. This name had been given her by the staff of the Fanling Babies' Home in Hong Kong when she had been found, a newborn infant, abandoned on the doorstep. But she had used her Chinese name for the last time. On an October day in 1954, Tak Oi Shi became Susan Lawrence Skinner, fifth child of the Lawrence Skinner family of Tacoma, Washington.

The story of Susie Skinner really began sixty years ago when two young Chicago medical students dedicated their lives to missionary service in China. In 1897 James E. and Susan Lawrence Skinner arrived at the port of Foochow, in the province of Fukien on the South China coast. For forty-eight years the Skinners worked in Fukien. Two boys were born there, grew up with an understanding of the people, their language and customs. Lawrence, the youngest child, is now Dr. Lawrence Skinner of Tacoma, father of a little girl once known as Tak Oi Shi.

I played with the Skinner children when I was a child,

was treated and nursed by the Doctors Skinner through many years of my childhood. The elder Skinners left China, as my own parents did, during the late years of World War II. A few years ago Dr. J. L. Skinner, left a widower, made his home with Dr. Lawrie and family in Tacoma.

As the communist tide engulfed mainland China, Dr. J. L. Skinner felt more than most people the tragedy that had come to his beloved China. The Skinners read of the swelling refugee tide reaching Hong Kong, of hordes of hungry children roaming the streets of Kowloon. And they wondered if among the weary refugees there might be old friends from Fukien Province. They wondered, too, how they might help.

Gradually a thought took form. Perhaps they could find an orphaned child, even one from Fukien, adopt her and bring her up as their own. Without knowing that the others had similar thoughts, members of the family had already named their orphan: she would be another Susan Lawrence Skinner.

So it was that in January, 1953, the Skinner family, all three generations, began to talk and plan. I am ashamed to say that when Dr. J. L. Skinner wrote me at that time, asking me—recently returned from the Far East—to give guidance, I thought of the tremendous difficulties involved and replied that the project was all but impossible. I had forgotten that for Dr. J. L. Skinner, whose life had been spent doing impossible things in the South China mountains, nothing was impossible.

In the summer of 1953, Dr. Skinner, then in his eighty-fifth year, traveled to Hong Kong to select the child, to begin the long fight through the labyrinths of red tape, State Department regulations and international laws. I am indebted to the Skinner family for allowing me the privilege of reading Dr. Skinner's letters written during the summer of 1953, and for access to many other facts about the battle to find Susie. Other facets of the story I have picked up myself at the Fanling Babies' Home in Hong Kong; for Susie has become the Home's most famous alumna.

On July 30th, 1953, Dr. Skinner wrote his family in Tacoma. "The orphanage authorities showed me four girls. There are no Fukien orphans here, only Cantonese. I picked out two I thought the nicest. They are girls brought in without history or background, between six and seven years old, bright-looking. I wonder if you will ask Dr. Walter Judd to intervene in Washington and start the wheels rolling."

Within a week Dr. Skinner had made his choice and forwarded pictures to Tacoma. In mid-August he wrote, "I am anxious to hear from you and know how she struck you. People will of course say you are foolish to try this, but I think her coming will be a blessing to all of us. I shall try to start her in English. . . ."

A week later, Dr. Skinner had encountered the first of many legal difficulties. "I'm just back from a talk with the American Consul. . . . He had just received word from Washington about orphans. But these regulations apply only to American servicemen abroad. That lets you out. There is another Act which will admit five thousand war orphans under ten years of age, but we do not know the requirements."

Meanwhile, back in Tacoma, tongues had begun to wag. Dr. Skinner wrote his family on September 1st, saying, "I am not surprised over the general disapproval of our plan. . . . I plan to go out to Fanling tomorrow and stay several days. I will then tell you if there is any fear on her part. I feel sure there will be none."

A few days later Dr. Skinner reported, "When I came to the compound the kids saw me and began to yell 'Tak Oi, Tak Oi.' They took me by the hand and we soon found her. I brought out the pictures, and the nurse told her in Chinese who each one was, and she was absorbed by it all. . . . The way the other children act when I come, you can be sure the excitement will spread to her. . . . When I left, Tak Oi went with me to the bus station. The last I saw of her she was waving good-bye. . . . I wrote the name Jean on a piece of paper, and she made a fair attempt at copying it. Then I wrote 'Susan,' told her this would be her name. She copied that better. One thing is sure, she is not the emotional type, will not be easily upset. I am sure you will love her, even though you cannot tell her that in words."

On October 14th, 1953, Dr. Skinner prepared to leave Hong Kong. He had filled in the various necessary forms, had secured the necessary pictures, had made numerous trips to Fanling and to the U.S. Consulate. With the help of Verent Mills of CCF, it appeared that Tak Oi would soon be on her way to America. He wrote his family on that day, "I saw the consul today. He called our problem the worst headache ever! He showed me the many letters they had received on the case. But he says it is now a sure thing and assured me I need not stay any longer on account of the girl. The orphanage folks think the plan to put her on a plane is a good one. They will send you word when to meet her in Seattle. . . . I leave here on the *Java Mail* on the 24th and will be home about November 8th."

Back in Tacoma, the Skinner family was excitedly awaiting the cable which would announce Susie's arrival.

Instead, nothing happened. It was then discovered that the War Orphan Act required that a child must have a Certificate of Readmission from the foreign country of origin. The British Government refused to grant the certificate, arguing that the girl's British passport would allow re-entry into Hong Kong any time during a five-year period, and that would have to suffice. There followed more months of haggling, of correspondence, of appeals to senators and representatives in Congress. The possibility of bringing Tak Oi in on a student visa was explored and dropped.

The only possible manner in which the little girl could enter would be for Congress to amend the Act, or to pass a special bill in her interest. An amendment had been written, but there was much controversial legislation before Congress; the amendment was ignored.

In August, 1954, Lawrie and Clara Skinner put Dad Skinner on a plane for Washington. His assignment was simply to agitate, to call on all the powers so that the amendment could be passed. It was a well-nigh hopeless job, for Congress was to adjourn in two weeks. But remember that nothing is impossible for J. L. Skinner. A frail, eighty-six-year-old man was able to force passage of the amendment to the Refugee Act only a few hours before Congress adjourned. The way was open at last.

So it was that Susan Lawrence Skinner, who once was known as Tak Oi Shi, moved into a house on Green Lane in the Tacoma suburbs. The neighbors watched with raised eyebrows. There were more comments about the foolish Skinners, taking in a child who could not speak a word of English!

But somehow the little waif, abandoned on the doorstep of a Hong Kong orphanage, understood the cataclysmic change that had taken place in her life. She had decided on a clean break from China. At the airport she refused to speak to the Chinese interpreter. Two months later, two Chinese students very much interested in her came to talk. She turned her back. She thrust out her jaw and scowled when a State Department photographer asked to take a picture of her in her lovely Chinese clothes (she had already posed willingly for pictures in her American clothes). She cried when the Skinners took her to a Chinese restaurant.

One day Clara Skinner showed Susie a picture of Verent Mills. "This is Reverend Mills, Susie. What is his Chinese name?" Instantly Susie replied, "Reverend Mills." It was months later when Mrs. Skinner was getting ready to tuck her into bed that she said, "Now I tell you Reverend Mills' Chinese name." And she did.

On one of the first nights of Susie's life with the Skinners, Mrs. Skinner showed her the laundry chute where she should put her soiled clothes. Susie made no move, looked at the dark hole with misgivings. Jean encouraged her, and reluctantly Susie let one sock fall into the chute. As the sock disappeared, the little girl knelt down and peered into the dark abyss. Suddenly she began to chatter to herself in Chinese (the only time she has ever spoken her own language since arriving in America). She was very much perturbed at the loss of her new sock. Dr. Skinner took her downstairs, showed her where the clothes emerged. Suddenly life was worth living again. Susie gathered up all the clothes she could carry, regardless of ownership, and headed back upstairs.

The next day it was necessary to go through the laundry chute routine again, step by step. Susie helped put the clothes in the chute, but with considerable suspicion. Then she helped put them into the washer, in the dryer.

Only when she knew with certainty that the clothes eventually reappeared, ironed and ready for use, would she accept this strange bit of American life.

Within two months of Susie's arrival the community had lost its skepticism, had taken her to its bosom. One mother commented, "Susie is the biggest thing that ever happened to Park Lodge School." The other children fairly adored her, crowded around her at recess, fought over the privilege of sitting next to her at lunch. From the beginning she was invited to every birthday party in the community.

No child ever began school under more handicaps. Her arrival at Park Lodge's first grade had come without any warning. The expression on Mrs. Venora Beecroft's face was one of utter amazement when Dr. Lawrie walked in with Susie. She knew one English word—"bathroom." But within a few months Susie became a star pupil, gifted with a remarkable ability to understand her new life.

After she had been in school a few months the class somehow became involved in a discussion of family relationships. One child observed that when he grew up and had babies he would be a father. Another child countered with the statement that when he grew up and his children had babies, he would be a grandfather. The teacher then took a hand and said to the class, "And when your grandchildren grow up and have babies, what will that make you?"

Susie, who had been following the discussion closely, timidly raised her hand. Shyly she answered Mrs. Beecroft, "Angel—yes?" At about the same time Susie approached Dr. J. L. Skinner one day, asking with interest, "Grandpa, why you not angel?"

There have been many adventures for Susie Skinner,

with more to come. American food was strange to her. At first she preferred vegetables to meat; now she prefers meat (including hot dogs, which have become a passion). She chews gum enthusiastically. She has little interest in dolls but will occasionally take her Easter bunny to bed with her because Jean does it and she thinks it must be the thing to do.

Susie has encountered a dentist for the first time, now looks forward to each visit. Her tonsils must be removed soon, and she is looking forward to this adventure with great anticipation, a tribute to the other Skinner children who have not enlightened her on the subject.

Susie was much intrigued by the playground equipment at school. She particularly loved the swings, obviously had never seen one before. During her first few weeks at school she was knocked down twice. After the first experience she hobbled about on crutches for several days—then promptly got in the way of a high swinger and was knocked unconscious. For weeks Susie was a menace to automobile traffic. She crossed streets without warning and without looking. Traffic just did not exist for her.

But Susie has now learned to ride her bike, to obey traffic regulations, to understand the difference between a red light and a green light.

As I write this, Susie has been in America for eighteen months. Clara and Lawrie Skinner are delighted with her progress. She has become a valuable addition to the church, the school, the whole community.

But Clara Skinner has some reservations about the Americanization of Susie. The oriental restraint, the beautiful behavior will soon be memories. At first Susie was quiet and ladylike, her manners perfect. There was no nonsense about doing important chores first. Now Susie giggles just like any other American girl. She has even been sent out of the room at school, to sit in the hall. At first she folded her clothes carefully on a chair at night, arranged her shoes underneath. "Now," says Clara Skinner, "her housekeeping leaves much to be desired—as does Jean's."

"I no longer feel that we are necessarily on the right track when it comes to a way of life," Mrs. Skinner wrote me recently. "But at least we are on a track, and Miss Susie is an enthusiastic passenger on the journey. She will be an American if it kills her."

But for Susie there are no reservations. The nameless baby, left on the doorstep of an orphanage in Hong Kong eight years ago, has found her heaven.

The Refugee Relief Act which has made Susie's heaven possible expires at the end of 1956. Perhaps it will be renewed. Only a small portion of the children who could have entered America under the provisions of the Act have benefited from it. From Hong Kong there have been a half dozen, perhaps 300-odd mixed-blood children from Japan, a trickle from Korea, from the countries of Europe.

While I share, at times, Clara Skinner's misgivings about some phases of the American way of life, I would like to see more Susie Skinners among us. The life that America offers is in truth a heaven compared to the life that most of the abandoned children of the world face. The children can also make a contribution, as Susie has, to our life. No child in America has been more closely watched by her neighbors than has Susie. And I doubt if there is a person in Tacoma who now doubts that Susie has been good for Tacoma.

But the simple fact is that there can be but a very few children like Susie Skinner. Even if the Refugee Relief Act is extended, only a tiny trickle of orphans can be legally adopted by American families. There are nations which do not want to lose their children, who place obstacles in the way of legal adoption. There is a maze of red tape, American and otherwise, that must be unraveled. And there are not many Americans willing to go abroad as Dr. J. L. Skinner did, personally to battle for a child's life.

I will not again, as I did in 1953 when Dr. Skinner wrote me for help, discourage any American family from attempting a legal adoption. But I do know that for every Susie Skinner there are ten thousand or twenty thousand children who cannot find their heaven in America.

Yet Americans can help the children find a heaven of lesser beauty, where the streets may not be paved with gold but are at least passable. There are numerous organizations doing work with children abroad; contributions to them will help the scores of thousands who cannot hope to reach our shores. Most Protestant denominations, as well as the Catholic Church, operate orphanages. Even in Riutula, northernmost home in the world, I found Care at work, supplying butter and other commodities.

There are several organizations which use the sponsorship or foster-parent plan, and these I recommend especially. For an orphaned child needs more than butter, more than an occasional gift of money or old clothes. Continuity of giving, month by month, can help children everywhere to a decent chance in life.

Foster Parents' Plan for War Children, Inc., with headquarters at 43 West 61st Street, New York, and the Save the Children Federation, United Nations Plaza, New York, are the two organizations, in addition to the Christian Children's Fund, most active in the field. Foster Parents' Plan operates by enlisting sponsors who pay $15 a month, Save the Children's Federation $10 a month.

Both organizations are active in Europe and Korea. Save the Children's Federation also has a program in the Middle East. As far as I have been able to ascertain, neither organization works in Japan or among Chinese, in Hong Kong, Formosa or Southeast Asia, in the Philippines or in India or Latin America.

Save the Children Federation does not work with orphans or with children's institutions. Its help goes to children living with their families, providing for clothing, food and schooling. SCF helps numerous schools, has 4-H type activities in rural areas. Foster Parents' Plan helps children who may or may not be orphans.

There are numerous other organizations, some regional. American Middle East Relief, Inc., provides emergency relief in Arab countries, helps promote self-help projects. Much of its work is beneficial to the many needy children among the refugee Arab population.

These are reputable organizations giving needed help that is properly administered. Unfortunately there are also organizations that are not reputable nor efficiently administered. It is possible to check on the nature of any organization claiming to help children overseas by writing the Advisory Committee on Voluntary Foreign Aid, Department of State, Washington.

I believe also it is wise to ask any organization which solicits funds for a copy of its financial statements. If administrative expenses run more than fifteen to eighteen per cent of total donations, the organization cannot, in my opinion, be considered efficient.

I believe the help that counts most is that which is given,

continuously over the years, to children in well-managed homes. Orphan children are supposed to suffer from emotional and psychological problems and undoubtedly do. It was not merely native ability that made Susie Skinner able so quickly to fit herself into an American family and educational system (after four months she could read better than two thirds of the children in her class). Susie has native ability and assets, to be sure. But she also had seven years of intelligent, loving care in the Fanling Babies' Home. The foundation had been laid, whether for life in America or life in Hong Kong.

It is significant that the graduates of Hong Kong's CCF-supported orphanages can obtain jobs without help from the traditional Chinese middleman, without the traditional guarantor. The foundations for responsible living are built and are often firmer than those of boys and girls from unbroken homes.

All over the world I encountered heartening success stories of boys and girls who had been abandoned as Susie was, or who had been plucked off the streets. In the heart of the Borneo jungles I found a product of the Christian Herald Industrial Home of Foochow, China; now the dean of a school, recently returned from study in England on a British Government scholarship. Added to the fact that this young man was brought up in an orphanage is the fact that he has been forced to leave his homeland, to build a new life as a refugee in a land far from home.

No child can begin life with any greater obstacles than do the outcaste children of India. Add to this initial hurdle that of being abandoned or without parents, and there is ample reason for emotional and psychological disturbance. Yet even among these children there are inspiring stories of success, women like Sara Daniel, orphaned outcaste child who is now a practicing physician in Saudi Arabia. There is probably no one from the depressed classes of India who has attained the financial success of "Little Paulose," one of the first ten orphans taken into the Alwaye Settlement. Paulose is superintendent of the nursing staff of a large oil company hospital in Iran. He has married a nurse and is able not only to raise a family of his own, but to give his sister's children in India a fine education.

It is possible to salvage the lives of thousands of children, to make those lives meaningful and worth while. But the job requires more than a gift of an old suit of clothing, a few dollars dropped into the collection plate, a can of surplus butter or milk. These gifts help temporarily, but they cannot alone build the needed foundations.

The greatest challenge is to have a child of foreign blood actually living within one's family as in the case of Susie Skinner. Next to this is the challenge of adopting a child overseas, of helping month after month and year after year to build a foundation for life.

There is another aspect besides the human one. In these days it is common to equate almost every activity with the struggle to contain communism. But surely there can be no disagreement that the support by Americans of 2,100 orphans in Hong Kong is a telling answer to the stream of abuse that comes from Communist China. And in Cochin-Travancore, India, center of communist activity, the nearly two hundred orphaned and abandoned children of the depressed classes cared for in the Alwaye Settlement must cause even the communists to pause and think as they denounce America, the nation of capitalists and warmongers.

As I have traveled around the world, seeing what Americans are doing for the children who are victims of wars they had no part in causing, I have been reminded constantly of the words of the Chinese businessman in Hong Kong commenting on America's help to China's children: "Here for all to see is a bit of America's heart abroad."

I have written of children in faraway lands. But need knows no ocean boundaries, cruelty is not defined by color of skin nor confined to those who live in other lands. As in the hovels of Asia, there are children found starving in American homes, children who have been beaten, children who have inadequate clothing. In Puerto Rico there are extensive slums, mile after mile; in San Juan alone, a thousand children who should be in institutions. In the western United States there are thousands of Indian children who have no educational opportunity. And in the southern mountains, the Ozarks, the swamplands of the Deep South, there are children with many needs, but above all the need for love.

Most of the institutionalized children in our South come from broken homes. Sometimes the break is legal, neither parent wanting the encumbrance of child or children. Frequently the father is unknown or unwilling or unable to fulfill the responsibilities he deserts.

There is one great difference between these children and those across the seas. Once they find their way into an institution, they receive better care, and live in luxury unknown to the needy children of Asia. There are children's homes in America which have their own extensive and productive farm lands. Some even have swimming pools.

I visited one of these homes in the South and marveled at

the spic-and-span kitchen, the great walk-in freezer filled with food grown on the institution's farm. Hesitantly I asked the superintendent if sponsorship of his children was of any help. For this home spends $430 a year for each child's food; surely, I thought, the few dollars a month received from a sponsor could have little value.

"These children need more than good food," the superintendent told me. "Above all, they need love, a feeling of belonging. The money from a foster parent means little. But the letters, the gifts, the visits—these are things that money cannot buy. And these are things our children cherish."

There are children in America as truly homeless, as truly orphaned, as the little ones of Korea. Enlightened welfare laws make their lot more bearable; they find shelter in fine buildings. But they too need something more, something money alone cannot buy.